Lead Conversations that Count

# LEAD CONVERSATIONS THAT COUNT

## How Busy Managers Run Great Meetings

**CAROLYN ELLIS**

Rowntree Press

Published by Rowntree Press

First published in 2021 in Toronto, Canada

Copyright © 2021 by Carolyn Ellis

www.brilliancemastery.com

The moral rights of the author have been asserted.

All rights reserved. No part of this publication may be used or reproduced, stored in a retrieval system or transmitted, in any form or by any means without the publisher's prior written consent.

Every effort has been made to trace (and seek permission for the use of) the original source of material used within this book. Where the attempt has been unsuccessful, the publisher would be pleased to hear from the author to rectify any omission.

All inquiries should be made to the author.
hello@BrillianceMastery.com
www.BrillianceMastery.com

Edited by Jenny Magee

Designed and typeset by BookPOD

ISBN 978-1-7777079-0-3 (paperback)

ISBN 978-1-7777079-1-0 (e-book)

# Contents

Introduction  1

## PART ONE: WHY LEAD CONVERSATIONS THAT COUNT

Chapter One: Why This is a Problem  13

Chapter Two: Why Conversations Matter  31

## PART TWO HOW TO LEAD CONVERSATIONS THAT COUNT

Chapter Three: Calibrate  53

Chapter Four: Orient  79

Chapter Five: Understand  107

Chapter Six: Navigate  131

Chapter Seven: Transfer  161

Chapter Eight: Handling Hybrid Meetings  181

## PART THREE YOUR NEXT STEPS

Chapter Nine: Your COUNT Roadmap  197

Work With Me  205

About the Author  206

Gratitude  207

References  208

# Introduction

We've all been in meetings that felt like a total waste of time. Endless, back-to-back meetings that clutter up the calendar and leave the real work to pile up.

You know how they go.

Meetings called on issues that are better handled by email.

People in love with the sound of their own voices, drone on about something that should have taken a few minutes.

Ramblers disappear down rabbit holes over obscure, inconsequential issues.

Participants talk over each other while others check their electronic devices under the table.

Boring presentations that provide no opportunity to ask questions or share views.

Meetings run over time with unaddressed chunks of the agenda that lead to even more meetings.

You end the meeting more confused than when it started, frustrated that it was all talk and no action, just like so many before it.

When you're the leader of the conversation, these kinds of problems fall on your shoulders.

How do you handle things when people get unruly? Or is it you who talks endlessly, leaving no space for back-and-forth dialogue in your meeting?

Perhaps your recent promotion requires you to lead the discussion, but you feel like you missed the memo on how to leave people excited to do the work and meet again, rather than just relieved the meeting is over and done with. Or maybe you're a seasoned team leader working virtually because of the COVID-19 pandemic, and you need to find better ways to keep your people connected and engaged.

The latest research indicates that people's experience of meetings is not great. It's estimated that unproductive meetings waste more than $37B a year, and executives view more than 67 percent of meetings as failures (Dempsey, 2019). Beyond sitting in meeting rooms, there's all the preparation time beforehand; even a simple status update meeting can require up to four hours of groundwork.

The research also shows that what happens in the meeting isn't inspiring. Some 92 percent of workers admit they multitask in meetings – and it's even easier to do when meeting virtually.

## We Need to Do Better

In an increasingly complex and ever-changing world, it's clear we have some big problems to solve. The scope of challenges most organizations face is beyond the ability of any single individual to figure out. Add a global pandemic that has turned the way we work and live upside down, and you have a whole new level of complication.

Why do we need to do better?

We have a laundry list of big problems to deal with – and quickly. The term "wicked problem" was coined to describe "a problem that is difficult or impossible to solve because of incomplete, contradictory, and changing requirements that are often difficult to recognize. It refers to an idea or problem that cannot be fixed, where there is no single solution to the problem". (Wikipedia, 2021). From issues like climate change, systemic racism, social injustice, the emergence of new technologies, and rising incidence of mental health, these are challenges that impact us as individuals, communities, businesses, public agencies, and governments. And, of course, the pandemic.

The scale of change is mind-boggling and can be paralyzing. Solving big problems starts with a conversation – with people talking to and listening to one another. It begins with the ability to share perspectives, ask questions, and trust one another enough to get creative, courageous and committed to finding a solution – together.

> Solutions don't come to us.
> Solutions come through us.
>
> – *Matt Church*

This is where you, as a Conversation Leader, have a significant role to play.

## We Want to Do Better

Managers at all levels have a few things in common. You want to do good work. You want to feel confident, have an impact, and realize success. You want to contribute through promotion or take on new roles that stretch you personally and professionally.

There's plenty that gets in the way of these goals. Like an explorer cutting a path through a dense jungle, you have to continually battle to get more done, with fewer resources, and in less time. It's frustrating when priorities change, new edicts are handed down, and you're the one responsible for carrying through those new directions. It feels like you're racing to put out one fire after another. The idea of work-life balance seems like a fairy tale as there's so much going on.

Often our response to increasing pressure to do more with less is to adopt a tactical approach. You take another time management course, get a new kind of planner or aim for in-box zero. Perhaps you listen to podcasts about the latest in leadership, business or innovation. It's tempting to search for a quick-fix or magic bullet to tackle the gnawing anxiety of leading your team through change, let alone finding solutions to seemingly intractable problems.

Yet, we only find the solutions we seek when we look within and commit to developing self-awareness and emotional intelligence. Cultivating a deep, unshakeable yet resilient presence brings important safety and confidence to how we show up in our work and how we show up as Conversation Leaders.

Imagine you are part of a mountain climbing expedition, with each member tethered to one another and the leader. The rope provides security, comfort, and a path for climbing successfully to the summit. Yet if the expedition leader falters, takes a misstep, or is not conditioned to exertion at high altitude, the rope goes slack, and everyone feels it give way. An unprepared leader impacts everyone, triggering fears for their safety and threatening their ascent.

There are indeed obstacles to navigating in the world, yet unless we intentionally focus on cultivating greater self-awareness and clearing some of our inner obstacles, we fall short of the potential that we, and our teams, can unlock.

## We Need to Show Up Better

Whether through a weekly team status update, a quarterly retreat, or even a one-to-one discussion with a direct report, the Conversation Leader has an enormous impact on the trajectory of success. Your presence and preparedness affect everyone in your meeting – even before you speak.

The default choice for many meeting leaders preparing for their next discussion is to figure out an approximate agenda and wing it from there. Who has time to do anything else, right? You've already got a lot on your plate, so you'll figure it out when you get there.

But by taking even ten minutes to intentionally and consciously prepare to lead the discussion, you'll experience a huge difference in your confidence and ability to manage even the most gnarly topics. When you lead Conversations that Count, it's less about the content and more about the connection you deliver. It's less about what you talk about and more about how you show up and create the space and safety for great discussions to happen.

## Lead Conversations that Count

As a coach and facilitator for more than 20 years, I've learned that the first person you need to lead is yourself. Getting clear, purposeful, and aligned within yourself is a critical first step in influencing and inspiring others. Taking a few moments to get centred within yourself vastly improves your ability to listen and engage with those around you.

> *If you want to go fast, go alone. If you want to go far, go together.*
>
> *– African proverb*

The quality of your relationships is a huge determinant of the quality of work you can do together. Certain ingredients will make your next conversation truly count and not just fade into irrelevance as with so many meetings before.

## What's Possible?

Deciding to lead Conversations that Count isn't about adding one more thing to your already crowded to-do list. Instead, it's an invitation to transform how you do the work and the possibility of feeling more freedom and confidence. It's about striking a balance between data and decisions with the hearts and humanity of everyone in the meeting room.

Just imagine how that would be.

Meetings when nobody says anything useful? That's a thing of the past.

Discussions where folks dive down into rabbit holes and pull the agenda off course? That hasn't happened for ages either.

Your discomfort at doing this "soft skills" thing and decoding the complexities of group dynamics? Now, you enjoy going up the learning curve! You welcome the unexpected and know you can shift any moment of discomfort or failure into an opportunity for insight and continued connection.

There is much that needs to change, and we must start somewhere. Having a great conversation that sparks new ideas and nurtures people's sense that we're all in this together is a wonderful way to begin.

Can you imagine a world where you felt joy the next time you scheduled a team meeting? Excited anticipation? A feeling that you couldn't wait to be in a room leading a conversation with colleagues and direct reports that you knew would be indispensable to your organization's success?

Today, more than ever, we need to find a way to make meetings matter. And this book will show you how to do so.

You're stepping into power and authority when you're at the front of the room. When facilitating a meeting, there is a delicate balance between creating the environment for rich, authentic dialogue to happen among participants and your ability to skew or direct the conversation.

Whether you're leading conversations for a large gathering of 100 or more, a small group of five to ten people or even a one-to-one discussion with a colleague, the principles are the same. Busy managers have little time to spare, so you can't find the bandwidth to take lots of additional workshops or facilitation training to help you improve your confidence and capability to make your next meeting matter.

## How Will This Book Help You?

I've designed the book to be picked up before your next meeting – to give you a new idea or approach, and implement it quickly. It is content-agnostic, so it doesn't matter whether you're leading a weekly team meeting or an annual strategic retreat. Leading Conversations that Count is about equipping you, as the leader of that discussion, to be prepared and attuned to some of the people dynamics you'll encounter and need to manage.

In **Part One**, we'll examine why it's essential to strengthen our ability to have a constructive discussion, debate and decision-making process. Busy lives, more work to do in less time and with fewer resources, and more distractions make it hard to do our best thinking. Yet creativity, resilience and persistence have never been more needed. I'll introduce you to Conversations that Count and show how great meetings can transform your team.

**Part Two** explains the five building blocks to leading Conversations that Count. Here you'll learn about the COUNT model, a framework for busy people to lead great meetings and discussions.

**Part Three** brings it all together. As I often say, information without action is useless, while information with action becomes wisdom. We'll zoom out and walk through the COUNT Roadmap. This is a valuable tool to complete even in just ten minutes before starting your meeting. It's how you prepare yourself to show up as a fully present, resilient and inspiring leader of the discussion. It's the final tool you can use to readily put what you've learned into action in a way that feels authentic and true to you.

Use this book to elevate your meetings from mundane to meaningful, and help draw people together to get great work done.

Let's get to it!

Organizations of every kind are facing rapid and unrelenting change. We, as a society, are facing systemic challenges and problems that are gnarly, complex and require our very best collective thinking to find potential solutions. If you think COVID-19 was the most disruptive issue in your lifetime, just wait until the impacts of global warming become more prevalent and severe.

In this Part, you'll learn the definition of Conversations that Count and why it's important to level up from meetings that are inconsequential and just more clutter in your busy day, to meetings that are truly indispensable gatherings that shift a team into greatness.

Let's get started.

# CHAPTER ONE

# Why This is a Problem

> The pace of change will never be slower than it is today.
>
> – Beth Comstock

## Good Intentions, Poor Execution

Tom was nervous. He was gathering with other senior leaders from his company for their annual summit. The stakes were high for bringing this global brain trust together in one room for some serious problem-solving. Tom's company was facing significant disruption to their business model and market in the financial services sector. Traditional business lines were falling short of their goals, and Tom had to work harder than ever to meet the targets for his division. It felt like the ground he used to stand on so confidently – and that led to his promotion – was turning into quicksand. He hoped this two-day retreat would provide some clear answers and new strategies to address the market and organizational challenges that were everywhere.

To add to these complex challenges, the company also wanted to figure out why their latest engagement scores were so disappointing. No expense was spared in hiring outside consulting experts to unpack the pattern of declining employee engagement at the firm and do in-depth research with employees. The CEO and exec team weren't happy with the results, which showed productivity flagging and staff turnover increasing. The reports identified a pervasive aversion to risk-taking and speaking up, and individual contributors were reluctant to go beyond the essentials of their job description. The research showed that people weren't motivated or taking responsibility for results. It also uncovered a lack of innovation and risk-taking skills that senior leadership felt necessary to tackle strategic challenges.

Large exhibits surrounded the meeting space, with colour charts, tables, photos and quotes gathered by the engagement research company displayed like a full museum exhibition. Senior leaders were here from all over the globe – the budget for costs of travel, accommodation and meals were hundreds of thousands of dollars, let alone the opportunity cost of taking these key performers away from their regular duties for the better part of a week. The stakes were high, and it was time for an honest, let-your-hair-down discussion about what the people and leadership of this organization needed to do to adapt and respond to a challenging and changing future. Tom felt pressured to justify how such disappointing engagement results were happening on his watch and with his unit.

The key agenda item was to find solutions through a brainstorming and feedback session with senior leadership. To do this, participants broke into smaller discussion groups. As a senior leadership team member, Tom was proud to be selected to lead a group. "It's showtime!" he thought, psyching himself up.

"We're here today to get real, to get deep, and really figure out how to turn around these engagement scores," Tom told his group of 30 people. "Solving that issue will unlock the kind of teamwork, creativity and results we need. What's going on with engagement, and how can we do better? So, I want to hear your ideas. Who wants to go first?" As he heard the words coming out of his mouth, Tom thought, "Yep, that's just the right tone, and I feel like I'm ready to drive this bus. I've got this!"

A few individuals spoke up with their ideas.

*"We have so many generations now at work, and we seem to have different priorities about how to do our work."*

*"There are too many silos out there now; it's hard to keep communication clear and timely."*

*"We need to revamp our performance assessment practices."*

As ideas slowly bubbled up from the group, Tom felt he had the discussion in hand. Some good ideas surfaced, and people were talking – even passionate. "This is going great," thought Tom. "No big surprises or land mines so far, so I'm doing really well!"

After about ten minutes of discussion, Sandra, a senior leader from the west coast office, raised her hand. "Why are we not more involved in strategic planning? It seems like we just hear about it afterwards from HQ. I think it would be helpful if a broader group of people across the company could be more involved in that important process." There was a murmur of acknowledgement in the group. A few heads started nodding in agreement.

Tom didn't understand the point Sandra was making. He felt the group had just hit a big pothole and Sandra's suggestion risked taking the discussion off-topic. He knew the importance of keeping focused on the stated agenda item of engagement. In an instant, Tom flashed back to many meetings where the discussion leader had let people ramble endlessly or take the group into rabbit holes. Truth be told, her idea hit a nerve with him because even though he wasn't involved in strategic planning, Tom didn't want to signal anything that might undermine his authority in the group.

Tom decided he needed to shut down this meandering, and his response was swift. "We are not here to talk about strategic planning. We are here to talk about engagement! They are different issues altogether," he said firmly, raising an eyebrow at Sandra. "Engagement is the most important issue we should be talking about now." He sighed, satisfied he had put Sandra in her place, and looked to the group for more discussion. "Phew!" he thought, "leading discussions can be like herding cats!"

Sandra took a half-step back, her eyes wide with shock at Tom's strong tone and volume. She thought this was supposed to be a brainstorming session. Feeling chastised, Sandra crossed her arms and shut down. The entire group fell silent. For a few seconds, you could hear a pin drop as everyone held their breath. Around Sandra, a few colleagues leaned in, nodding and whispering words of understanding.

Tom waited for the group to continue the discussion, but something was different now. The pit in Tom's stomach grew as nobody raised their hand or spoke up. People were silent and uncomfortable, looking around the room or at their feet. Few kept eye contact with Tom. He didn't understand why the energy had shifted in an instant, from engaged and involved to disengaged and distant.

Tom was confused and felt his throat tighten – this was a high-stakes problem. He wanted and needed their input to help find some solutions, but now all he was getting was the silent treatment. In his view, this entire group was clearly part of the disengagement problem they were supposed to be solving – after all, they weren't participating anymore. The few people who did finally speak up offered superficial suggestions without putting anything new on the table. Tom felt his impatience rise. The group's failure to provide concrete solutions would reflect on him, and he felt even more pressure over what to tell his boss once the session was over.

## Leading Conversations in a Pressure Cooker

If you've ever been responsible for leading a discussion, whether as part of your job description or taking your turn to run the next group meeting, you've been in Tom's shoes. Feeling the pressure to perform, finding a solution, and convinced that your team is more hindrance than help.

Sadly, you've likely been in Sandra's shoes as well. You show up ready to give your best and share your ideas and concerns, only to be shut down by an authority figure. Having the rug pulled out from under you like that (especially in front of others) makes you guarded, cautious, and think twice about how you will curate any future contributions to the group.

As the Conversation Leader, it's your responsibility to create an environment for your colleagues to do their best work. It's your job to lead what I call "Conversations that Count". These are discussions that strengthen relationships, clarify what's at stake and create the space for people to collaborate, create and do their best work together.

Before clarifying what these conversations are, let's take a brief look at what they are not. Tom's story provides several examples of how he fell short of the mark:

- Tom never **acknowledged** Sandra's point about strategic planning; he dismissed it outright.
- Tom didn't ask **questions** on the connection she saw between strategic planning and engagement. He felt confronted and shut it down instead of getting curious and exploring the point she was making.
- Tom's strong rebuke was contrary to the **agreement and format** he established of a brainstorming session to explore ideas and solutions. In so doing, the group's psychological safety evaporated and impacted the quality and health of the discussion.
- Tom's **communication and tone** were a mismatch for a collaborative session. While he may not have said it in so many words, his brusque energy and dismissive attitude delivered a clear message to Sandra and the entire group: "You're wrong. That's not what we're here to talk about. You better get back on track."

We've all been in rooms – whether in person or virtually – where the biggest conclusion was that it was an hour of your life you'll never get back again.

It's particularly frustrating when the person charged with the responsibility of leading the discussion doesn't do it well, or at all. They miss the essential dynamics of the group. They let pontificators consume all the air time and sabotage the agenda. On the one hand, they ask for feedback and blue-sky thinking (as Tom did) but then respond to that input with a closed mind or dismissive comments that shut down participation.

To be effective in business, you need to work with others, learning how to read the room, notice cues from participants and adapt on the spot. Much of that work requires creativity, diversity of thinking and focus. To bring all of those ingredients together in your next meeting or group discussion, you need to learn how to lead Conversations that Count.

## Dwindling Resources: Time and Attention

Good, old-fashioned conversation is becoming a scarce commodity in our modern world. In the course of the day, two resources are finite for all people: their time and attention.

Time is a non-renewable resource. Think of meetings and discussions where it feels as if your life force is ebbing away with wasted time. You can be highly skilled at time management, but you're behind the eight-ball unless you treat every minute with purpose, intention, and clarity.

People's attention is a limited resource that faces increasing demands in today's modern society. The ability to pay attention is a constant battle fought in the face of a daily barrage of social media, emails, texts buzzing, phone calls and more. In his book, *The Happiness Equation*, Neil Pasricha shares some indicators of the hamster wheel of daily decisions (Pasricha, 2016).

- We check our phones more than 150 times a day
- The average worker gets 147 emails a day
- There are 3.5B Google searches conducted daily
- We make an average of 295 decisions a day.

We use our attention differently and more intensively than our parents or grandparents did. Ron Miller argues that "Our attention isn't diminishing; it's becoming more demanding. It processes information increasingly intensively, and it's almost always hungry for more." (Miller, 2016).

How often have you heard about the latest and greatest Netflix series from a friend or a meme on social media, done some quick Google searches, and then found and binged the entire series within the week? (Surely, it's not just me, is it?)

Our attention is more easily driven by dopamine hits than by the need for deliberation and contemplation. Cal Newport, the author of *Deep Work* and *Digital Minimalism*, argues that our ability to do focused, deep and reflective work has been impacted by brains trained to react to distraction and addicted to short-term dopamine hits. "To simply wait and be bored has become a novel experience in modern life, but from the perspective of concentration training, it's incredibly valuable," argues Newport (Newport, 2016). Newport defines his notion of "deep work" as the ability to work in a state of deep concentration and focus for extended periods, without distraction or interruption, pushing one's cognitive capabilities to the limit. We might feel busy battling our way to in-box zero, but if it's at the expense of planning out your department's strategic priorities and challenges, there's a problem. Newport argues that the ability to perform deep work is a competitive advantage in a rapidly changing workplace. "Simply put, humans are not wired to be constantly wired." (Newport, 2019).

Overloaded with data and demands, the amygdala in our brain triggers a fight or flight response, flooding our brains with adrenalin and cortisol. In that state, it is challenging to access the pre-frontal cortex to think critically, assess, prioritize information, innovate and create.

Add to that mix the chronic, unpredictable stress of adapting to life in the COVID-19 pandemic. Dr Roger McIntyre, a professor of psychiatry and pharmacology, explains that this type of stress over a long period impacts brain regions that lead us to experience a "brain fog" where people feel more tired, less motivated and less joyful (McIntyre, 2021). We've lost the usual reference points and structures that guide our day. Wake up, go to work, come home, play with the kids or dog, eat, sleep and repeat.

We also now suffer from Zoom fatigue. Working from video conference platforms instead of face-to-face conversation requires our brains to work much harder to process non-verbal cues, such as expression, tone, pitch and body language. Our brains have been working overtime to decode meaning in communication in this new virtual world (Jiang, 2020).

## Defining Conversations that Count

Conversations that Count are discussions that make intentional and constructive use of your time and attention. They range from daily 15-minute stand-ups or weekly team meetings to brainstorming and project planning sessions and Town Halls. The principles of what makes a conversation count, engaging and inspiring people to do their best, can also be applied in one-to-one conversations.

Conversations that Count are built upon the following pillars:

- **Intention** – Conversations that Count are carefully designed, not rote. They are crafted to respect people's time and attention.
- **Relationship** – People and the way they connect and relate to one another are central. A Conversation that Counts helps to strengthen relationships and prioritizes people rather than process and procedures.
- **Ecosystem** – Conversations that Count are dynamic, not static. They are responsive and foster a participatory and psychologically safe space for all to be heard and seen.

What might be unleashed if you operated from the premise that every minute of people's time and attention needs to be earned? Those two components – time and attention – are at the core of distinguishing what makes a conversation count and what makes it a waste of time.

In Figure 1, which quadrant have you spent the most time in as a leader of a conversation? What about as a participant?

Was time well spent, meaningful returns in terms of clarity, alignment, creativity, decision-making?

How was people's attention? Were they engaged in the discussion? Did they participate and contribute? Did they have skin in the game?

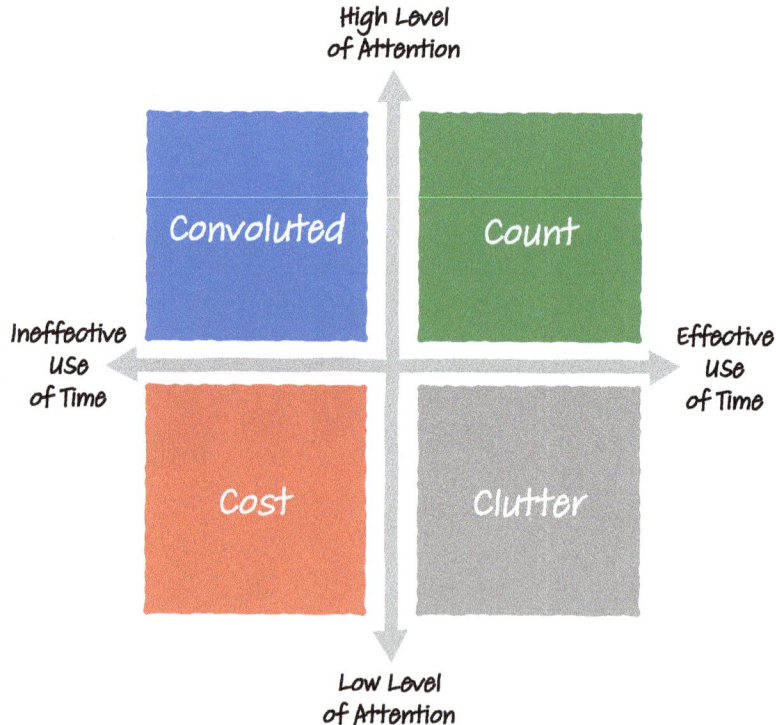

Figure 1: What Kind of Meetings Do Your Teams Have?

**Cost: Ineffective Use of Time and Low Level of Attention**

These meetings aren't well organized, lacking a clear agenda or desired outcomes. Participants aren't active and show up distracted. There is little intention to the meeting structure, and relationships are not well nurtured or even overtly considered in how the meeting is run.

**Clutter: Effective Use of Time and Low Level of Attention**

These meetings may be an efficient use of time, i.e. communicating to large groups through Town Halls, but provide little space for participant dialogue or engagement. Participants consume the message but have no time to contribute or apply it, so it is forgotten, ending up as clutter in calendars and people's mental bandwidth.

**Convoluted: Ineffective Use of Time and High Level of Attention**

These meetings have an important purpose that keeps participants' attention high because they have some stake in the game, yet the agenda design and meeting management are not well executed. Discussions about strategic direction or reorganization can fall into this category.

Processes are available to guide the discussion, but they aren't led effectively or customized to meet the needs of the group. People feel like the discussion rambles and that every diversion needs to be followed.

Being stuck in a group hamster wheel of discussion on important matters without structure or a way to make a decision can be very disconnecting, particularly when it happens in a virtual environment. Attention quickly erodes as participants have no meaningful way to influence or participate effectively in the discussion.

**Count: Effective Use of Time and High Level of Attention**

These meetings have a lasting impact. Just like the Goldilocks story, these meetings are just right. Not too long and tedious, and not so short and trivial that you wonder why you couldn't have read it in an email. What elevates a meeting into the Count quadrant is respect for people's time and leveraging attention so people feel heard, respected, and committed to making things happen. These meetings foster connection and relatedness between those in attendance, and there is a sense that everyone's voice matters.

## A Shift in Mindset

The beginning of any change requires first a shift in mindset.

Deloitte's 2021 Global Human Capital trends speak strongly to the need to shift from a "survive" mindset that many have adopted due to the drastic and swift changes required from COVID-19 to a "thrive" mindset to carry organizations into a perpetually changing future. "Organizational preparedness hinges on the ability to bring human strengths such as decision-making and adaptability to the fore, not just during a point-in-time crisis, but continually. It means taking the creativity unleashed by the need to survive a crisis – the creativity that is a hallmark of being human – and using it to reinvent the organization and its future. COVID-19 proved that people and organizations are capable of tremendous growth under the pressure of a crisis. The challenge for many will be to sustain that momentum to discover new ways to thrive in the long term, even as disruptions constantly reset the path forward." (Volini, et al., 2020).

> *What got you here won't get you there.*
> *– Marshall Goldsmith*

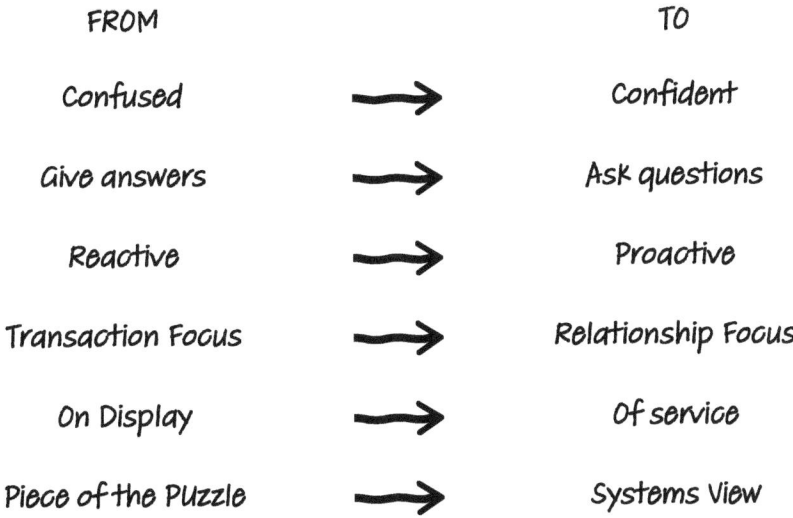

Table 1: Mindset Shifts for Conversation Leaders

The table above outlines possible shifts for you, as a manager or team leader, when leading a group of people in conversation.

**From Confused to Confident**

When beginning to run meetings, the emerging Conversation Leader may feel confused and even overwhelmed. New managers – particularly those promoted for their technical expertise – may feel out of their depth in navigating the world of interpersonal dynamics and social cues. Doing this in a virtual environment adds a whole new level of challenge and confusion to the mix.

The Conversation Leader will experience a greater level of confidence by applying the principles and following the stages of leading Conversations that Count. Part of that confidence comes from knowing it's not all about them. They learn there is a wealth of experience in the team that can be tapped and harnessed.

**From Giving Answers to Asking Questions**

The emerging Conversation Leader's first impulse is to have all the answers and give them freely to the group. This dynamic turns a discussion into a presentation. If you're not willing to have your ideas questioned, do you even need the meeting? You might as well send the group a video of yourself sharing your views.

When leading Conversations that Count, you'll become adept at asking questions, employing them as necessary tools to understand issues and perspectives at a deeper level, rather than as a signal that you don't know enough. Questions enable you to open up the discussion for more clarity. Weave them into the conversation to help the group make meaning together, be better able to empathize with each other, and explore assumptions, options and actions in a constructive way that fosters innovation and collaboration.

**From Reactive to Proactive**

Stress and time pressure combine here to create a reactive response. You may tend to shoot from the lip, creating unnecessary friction and uncertainty in the discussion. Leading discussions and navigating the complex world of human dynamics, differing opinions, and challenging problems may feel like you're stuck playing a game of whack-a-mole.

Once you learn how to lead Conversations that Count, you operate with a proactive mindset. You have a broader and more integrated perspective, and more readily pick up on important nuances, connections and potential pitfalls, and can respond thoughtfully or head them off before they erupt. You can look a few steps ahead and not get caught flatfooted.

**From Transaction Focus to Relationship Focus**

The novice Conversation Leader is very focused on getting the work done. The meeting is a means to an end, and that end is crossing things off your group to-do list and advancing your stated goals. The environment of the discussion tends to be more functional and process-oriented.

Using the Conversations that Count framework, the leader operates from the principle that the quality of relationships team members have with one another is hugely important to the team's success. More importantly, building a sense of connection inspires trust and engagement. Keeping a focus on relationship and paying attention to how you work together helps build sustainable success.

**From Feeling on Display to Being of Service**

When you begin leading meetings, there's an initial phase where you may feel your skills, appearance and capabilities are scrutinized and judged by everyone. You feel on display and self-conscious.

The leader of Conversations that Count starts from the premise that everything they do is of service. They ask, "How can I help you be successful?" rather than "How do I look?" They are willing to lead even when uncomfortable or uncertain because they realize it's not about them. Their role is to create an environment where their people can do and be the best.

**From Looking at a Puzzle Piece to a Systems View**

When starting, you know what you know and are often reluctant to leave that space of comfort. With expertise in a particular area, your understanding may be filtered through the one piece of the puzzle you know so well. This can lead to siloed thinking and an inability to see connections between issues or appreciate different perspectives.

The leader of a Conversation that Counts recognizes that individuals do not operate in isolation. These leaders step back to see the whole picture rather than responding to a single issue or individual. They take a systems view of how the meeting unfolds. The renowned statistician W. Edward Demming argued that 94 percent of worker performance issues had to do with the systems in which workers operate, not with individual workers themselves, writing, "People can't perform better than the systems allow" (Andrew, 2018).

Think of a mobile – a toy that many parents place over their baby's crib to keep them amused. Every piece is connected to a central structure. If you touch one part, the whole thing bobs up and down and turns and spins until it reaches a new equilibrium. The Conversation Leader is willing to look past potential "problem personalities" and explore the nuances and complexities of the bigger system in which they, and their team, operate.

## Take Action

###  Get to Know your Meetings

Think about the most impactful and least memorable meetings you've been part of. Review Figure 1 and consider how you would categorize these meetings. What were some of the most significant meeting mistakes you've experienced? How did they impact the meeting?

_____

_____

_____

_____

###  Give Yourself a Mindset Checkup

Choose two of the paired mindset shifts from Table 1 that feel most important to you. Where might you feel stuck in each, and what would be possible if you were to make the shift?

_____

_____

_____

_____

CHAPTER TWO

# Why Conversations Matter

*We rise by lifting others.*

– *Robert Ingersoll*

Let's rewind the Chapter One story of Tom and Sandra. What if Tom had had the tools to lead a Conversation that Counts with his team? Read on and notice the changed outcome of the discussion when he employs some of the COUNT principles you will learn in this book.

SANDRA: "Why are we not more involved in strategic planning? It seems like we just hear about it afterwards from HQ. I think it would be helpful if a broader group of people across the company could be more involved in that important process."

TOM: (Inner dialogue: *Why is she even talking about strategic planning when we're here to talk about engagement? Are these issues even related? Whoa! My heart just started pounding. I need to step back from just reacting and shift my mindset around this. I'll acknowledge her point and get curious.*)

TOM: "Sandra, what I hear you saying is that if the company changed its approach to strategic planning, it could help us solve the engagement challenges? Did I get that right?"

SANDRA: "Yes, that's what I'm saying."

TOM: "Great! I'm curious about that idea. Can you share more about why you think that opening up the strategic planning process in some way would impact employee engagement?"

SANDRA: "Sure! In my opinion, a big part of the problem in engagement is that people don't feel connected to their work. They don't know why we are even doing the work in the first place. Right now, strategic planning is the process where we set the priorities and directions, but there's really only a handful of people who sit at that planning table. The impact of that is the overall direction feels like it gets handed down from on high, and the rest of us are just expected to execute it and feel engaged in making it happen.

"But we don't have a voice in the priorities or directions. If we could create some kind of input into strategic planning, I think people would have a greater sense of buy-in to the overall direction. I think that would translate into having people more personally invested in achieving the goals they helped to form. I've been using a more collaborative and participatory approach in my business unit, and I'm seeing my team's engagement scores are higher than average. I think it's an idea worth exploring more broadly across the company."

TOM: (Inner dialogue: *Ah, I see now. I hadn't thought of that connection before! I'm glad she brought it up.*)

TOM: "Thanks for elaborating on that, Sandra! Do others feel that there's potential for broader involvement in the strategic plan to positively impact engagement scores? I see a lot of you nodding and raising your hands. Let's add that idea to our list of initiatives to explore. Does anyone else want to contribute something to this idea that Sandra has raised?"

Do you see how the outcomes could be quite different? By shifting his mindset to curiosity and asking Sandra to share more, Tom has ensured that he has created a space where people feel safe to share ideas that may have a different perspective or frame. By acknowledging Sandra, Tom has opened up a new understanding and greater collaboration within the group.

Which version of the scenario do you think stands a better chance of solving the problem of declining employee engagement?

## Why Aren't We Better at This?

It's not really Tom's fault that his tool kit for leading Conversations that Count is somewhat empty. Making that transition from strength in technical skills to leading, engaging, influencing, and navigating the complexity of human dynamics isn't simple at the best of times. The additional stress of living and working in a global pandemic and the huge shift in how we work together adds a whole new level of pressure and uncertainty.

There are many reasons Tom may be feeling and operating out of his depth.

### Lack of Training

He may not have had any training in the basics of facilitating group discussion. Professional development budgets aren't limitless and are often targeted at senior levels or identified rising stars. If Tom is stepping into greater responsibility for managing people, he may not have received adequate training to support his communication and people skills.

**Lack of Role Models**

Unfortunately, many people have far more poor examples than great ones of how to lead a discussion. Without positive role models or a mentor to provide personal assistance, Tom may struggle to find a real-life example to emulate. In that situation, meetings can become presentations where one person talks at a group of people – a grown-up version of the Show and Tell sessions you had in kindergarten with no opportunity for engaging, back-and-forth discussion.

**Lack of Experience**

Leading groups in discussion, or even having a more engaged one-to-one conversation, requires practice and experience. Tom may not yet have been able to get that kind of experience. Like learning to raise a child, you can read all the books about how to be a great parent, but when your child is in your arms, it's a whole different ball game. Your baby, toddler and teen haven't read those books. You truly learn by doing. As your child progresses through their developmental stages, so do you as a parent. The experience you gain from making choices, learning from what worked and what didn't, and giving and receiving feedback from your child helps hone your competency and strength as a parent. The fundamental relationship you have as parent and child is constantly evolving and will inform you more than a whole library of how-to books, online parenting forums, or advice sessions with fellow parents.

**Need to Strengthen Soft Skills**

Tom's demonstration of technical expertise got him promoted to a role where he now needs to lead his group. He may not be fully convinced of the need to develop his emotional IQ or people skills. His mindset will be crucial to his development. Carol Dweck, the author of *Mindset: The New Psychology of Success,* explains that "our mindset shapes our beliefs in accomplishing something. People with a fixed mindset believe they are born naturally gifted at doing some things but utterly incapable of others, whereas people with a growth mindset believe they can become virtuosos of anything if they try hard enough" (Dweck, 2007).

**The Fear of Failure**

Climbing the learning curve in front of people you work with (particularly those who report to you and expect your leadership and wisdom) isn't easy. For Tom, the stakes feel high, and the pressure is on. There is a level of exposure and vulnerability when you don't feel fully confident or even competent in a task you are expected to perform. Tom may fear a risk of failure that could blunt or derail his professional career path.

**Preparing for the Skills of Tomorrow**

The World Economic Forum published reports in 2016 and 2020 on the top job skills needed for the future, based on extensive surveys with global employers. It predicted that half of us would need to reskill in the next five years, given the double disruption of the pandemic's economic impacts and increasing automation transforming jobs.

The top skills of critical thinking and problem-solving have remained consistent since the first report in 2016. But self-management skills are now emerging, such as active learning, resilience, stress tolerance and flexibility (World Economic Forum, 2020).

**Top 10 skills of 2025**

- Analytical thinking and innovation
- Active learning and learning strategies
- Complex problem-solving
- Critical thinking and analysis
- Creativity, originality and initiate
- Leadership and social influence
- Technology use, monitoring and control
- Technology design and programming
- Resilience, stress tolerance and flexibility
- Reasoning, problem-solving and ideation

**Type of Skill**
- Problem-solving
- Self-management
- Working with people
- Technology use and development

**Source:** Redesign from the Future of Jobs Report 2020, World Economic Forum.

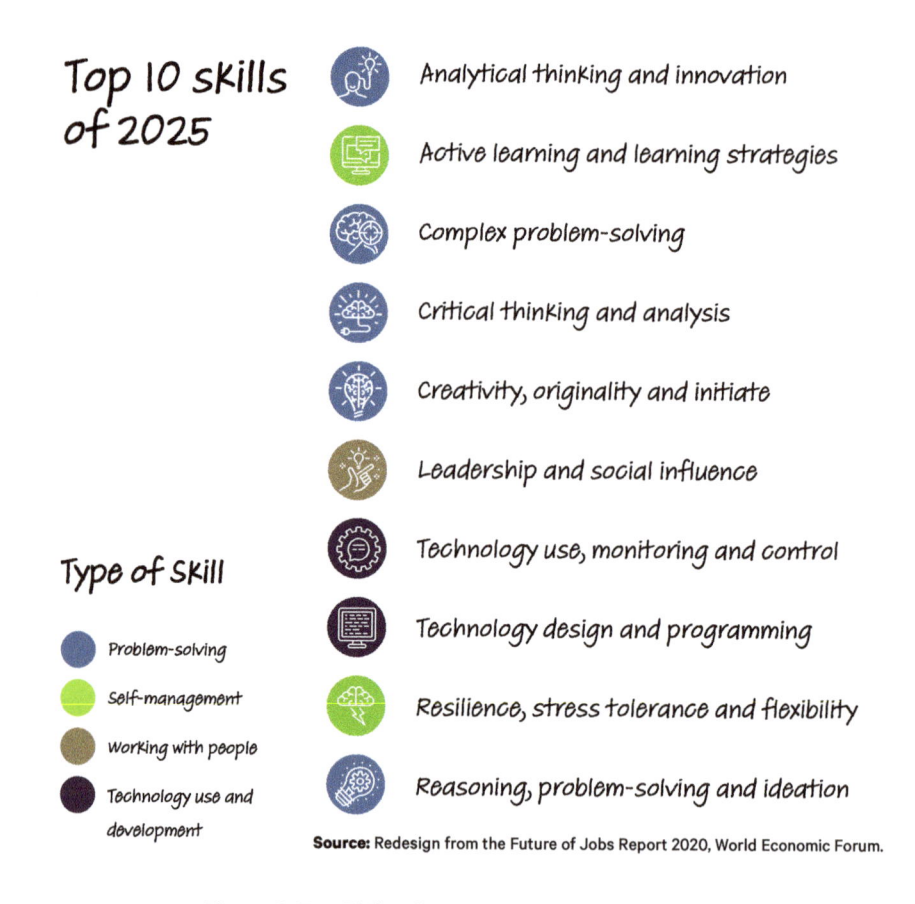

Figure 2: Top Skills of 2025 (World Economic Forum)

So many of these skills come together when you lead a Conversation that Counts. Notice that basic skills of time management or productivity aren't on this list. In fact, many speak to the dynamics of how people work and communicate together, even more than the content or issues. It is increasingly important to know how to tune in to the energy and shifting dynamics of working in groups.

> Change will not come if we wait for some other person or some other time. We are the ones we've been waiting for. We are the change that we seek.
>
> – *Barack Obama*

## Working Virtually – Raising the Stakes in Creating Conversations that Count

There has been a massive shift in how organizations work since the COVID-19 pandemic was declared in March 2020. As the virus spread, all sectors of industrialized economies that were not on the front lines of diagnosing and combatting the virus had to change how their teams worked. Almost overnight, employers asked their employees to work from home.

Ensuring platforms and equipment were available to enable this was a steep learning curve. The videoconference platform Zoom experienced an explosion in demand, growing from an average of ten million daily meeting participants in December 2019 to 350 million by December 2020 (Molla, 2020). It has become such a ubiquitous means of communication and connection that the word zoom is now a verb, as in "Zoom you later!"

The learning curve for employees working from home was also steep, particularly as the pandemic impacted schools. Working parents struggled to support their children with online learning as schools closed and classrooms became virtual. Schools re-opened then closed again, based on recommendations of the public health officials monitoring the spread of the virus. In some jurisdictions, school boards offered hybrid options where parents could choose either in-person or virtual instruction for their children. Being a parent, worker, educator and on-call 24/7 for child care is a juggling act many continue to do successfully.

Even as COVID-19 vaccines roll out, it seems clear that the pandemic has indelibly changed the way we work and gather. From large corporate offices to the local corner retail store, businesses have been retro-fitted to include physical barriers and measures to ensure social distancing. Rotating work schedules are being adapted to allow less staff onsite than at pre-pandemic levels. The "next normal" is still unfolding at the time of writing, with hybrid meetings, shifts in employee work patterns, and changes in consumer behavior reshaping the business landscape in lasting ways. As virus transmission rates rise or fall, the need to continually adjust seems to be part of the landscape for workplaces.

There are important differences when leading a virtual conversation instead of in-person meetings.

**Experience: Collective vs Individual**

When together in person, it's easier to create a sense of being part of a group with a collective and shared purpose. Conversation Leaders need to pay greater attention to building connection and trust in each other when working virtually. It's especially true when your organization brings on team members who may only have met their new colleagues via a video conference.

**Rapport: Organic vs Designed**

Building rapport comes naturally in a boardroom, where you can socialize and get to know each other personally. You can see Mahmoud's latest addition to his famous sock collection or offer quiet condolences to Trish on her father's passing. While those spontaneous touchpoints as you get coffee or take your seats may seem inconsequential, they provide myriad connection opportunities between the team.

In a virtual setting, you can't assume rapport will happen. It has to be designed and crafted, particularly when the agenda is packed. As you don't want to ask people to be on hours of videoconferences, it's easy to prune out unproductive time that doesn't focus on the issues at hand. Author and trainer Chad Littlefield advocates "Connection before content" (Wise & Littlefield, 2017).

**Distractions: Few vs Frequent**

It's easy to manage distraction in your workplace. Typically, you'll gather in a designated meeting space, with audio-visual equipment, flipcharts, whiteboards, and wall space as needed. One of the most powerful pieces of equipment in your meeting space is a door, which may even have a sign indicating "Meeting in progress" to ward off unwanted distractions or interruptions.

Contrast that with the environment your team members may have when working at home. Some may have an office where they create a sense of separation from their home environment. Some may not. Many will share their environment with other household members – spouses, children, roommates, pets – whose busy and active schedules can create a distraction. The ability to block out distractions or interruptions is not a given, and worrying about potential interruptions or technical glitches can erode your focus and attention.

Even the space of the virtual meeting – your computer screen – is rife with distractions. After all, you can look like you're paying attention, but you can easily quickly check your email, right? (C'mon now, we've all done that!) And perhaps you can google that new restaurant you heard about that delivers food. What was the name of it again? Better dive into Facebook to dig that up quickly. The temptation to veer out of the virtual meeting space and into numerous other distractions is at your fingertips. As the Conversation Leader, the battle to get – and keep – your participants' attention is tough and ongoing.

**Energy: Enlivening vs Draining**

When meeting with others, if one person's energy starts to dip, it's possible to feel inspired and encouraged by the others in the room. Neuroscience supports the fact that our brains are wired for connection and social interaction. According to Dr Jena Lee, "Social interactions are very much associated with our reward circuits, as oxytocin – the hormone involved in social bonding – modulates the same dopaminergic pathways involved in reward processing…So more active social connection is associated with more perceived reward, which in turns affects the very neurological pathways modulating alertness vs fatigue."

You can look people in the eyes, read cues from body language or tone of voice, and establish the context to understand where they are coming from. You're not alone, and there is a collective spirit you can tap into. Of course, there are those meetings where you can feel dragged into the mire when the group's energy starts to slide or get chaotic. Nonetheless, being in others' presence helps tap into potential synergies and the idea that the whole is greater than the sum of its parts.

When working virtually, your connection is limited to a small box in a "Brady Bunch" view of individual faces on a computer screen. While the brain loves in-person social interactions, it has to work harder in video conferences, Lee notes. Audio delays are associated with more negative perceptions and distrust between people. It takes greater cognitive effort to decode non-verbal cues in a virtual environment.

"Without the help of these unconscious cues on which we have relied since infancy to socioemotionally assess each other and bond, compensatory cognitive and emotional effort is required. In addition, this increased cost competes for people's attention with acutely elevated distractions such as multitasking, the home environment (e.g. family, lack of privacy), and their mirror image on the screen." (Lee, 2020). Working from home has also made us sedentary, which in itself brings a risk of higher fatigue.

## The Impact of Leading Conversations that Count

Your impact when leading a conversation lies along a continuum. Learning to decipher and work with group dynamics may come naturally to some, while it feels like an impossible skill to others. We learn by doing and through our own experience. Many managers who have risen through the ranks on the virtue of their technical skills may find themselves in unknown territory. Leading Conversations that Count requires a blend of emotional intelligence, self-awareness, strong listening and communication skills, and a willingness to be uncomfortable – all in front of a room where the eyes are on you, and the responsibility for leading the team is yours.

If you've been to an orchestra live in concert, you'll have seen the conductor guiding and shaping the performance. He or she undoubtedly has skills and experience in one, or perhaps more, musical instruments. But their expertise is in guiding each section of the orchestra to create an experience that interprets the composer's score harmoniously. The responsibility for timing, volume, cueing in soloists, and weaving individual contributions into an outstanding performance lies with the conductor being able to draw out the best from individual orchestra members.

| Conversation Leader's Capability | Impact on Team | Meeting Effectiveness | Team Productivity |
|---|---|---|---|
| CAPABLE | SHIFT | INDISPENSABLE | 10x |
| COMPETENT | LIFT | IMPACTFUL | 5x |
| CAUTIOUS | SIFT | INFORMATIONAL | 1x |
| CARELESS | RIFT | INDISCRIMINATE | -5x |
| CLUELESS | ADRIFT | INCONSEQUENTIAL | -10x |

Table 2: The Impact of Leading Conversations that Count.

To get started, take a look at Table 2, which outlines a spectrum of impact Conversation Leaders can have. At which stage are you and your team now? Where would you like to be? In Part 2, you'll close the gap by learning the ingredients of successfully leading Conversations that Count.

**Inconsequential**

At this level, the conversations themselves have minimal impact on the team's ability to get its work done effectively and productively. It's as though you are a guitar player whose guitar sits collecting dust in the attic. The thought of leading group meetings, especially those that deal with contentious or complex issues, may make you feel queasy and clueless. Where do you start?

Having a title of responsibility or authority doesn't automatically make you a competent leader of others. I've encountered people who relentlessly delegate issues, feeling they are empowering their team. The consequence can be that the team feels unsupported rather than delegated, having been passed the "hot potato" from their manager. Set adrift, they risk becoming cynical and distrusting.

At this level, conversations feel more like a waste of time than an opportunity to tap into the team's collective wisdom to share knowledge and solve emerging issues together.

**Indiscriminate**

At this level, the Conversation Leader realizes their role in running team meetings, but their approach is inconsistent. Their leadership is influenced by the latest "how to run a meeting" article or a tip from a colleague. Like an inexperienced piano player learning to play a basic tune, the Conversation Leader employs a few key tactics to manage group dynamics or run the meeting, but the conversation stays relatively superficial. The leader is somewhat careless in attending consistently to different perspectives within the group or emerging issues brought to the table. It's a classic situation of "If all you have is a hammer, then every problem looks like a nail."

The impact on the team is to create a rift. Trust drops, and cynicism rises. The haphazard response and support from the leader erode the ability of the group to work effectively together.

**Informational**

At this level, the leader has some self-awareness of their role and responsibility to create an environment for the team to have effective meetings and discussions. Like the piano player starting to understand the basics of time signatures, musical theory, or playing simple chords, there is a limit to the Conversation Leader's comfort zone. This leader runs meetings with a degree of caution, keeping discussion within the parameters of common interest and understanding. They influence and persuade by defaulting to reliance on objective facts and data.

They might have risen through the ranks on technical expertise, yet their emotional intelligence and ability to read the room aren't strongly developed, which further feeds their sense of caution. Like the Titanic captain who thinks it's enough to steer his ship around the visible tip of the iceberg, the leader avoids handling the more subtle and complex emotional and interpersonal dynamics that may lie beneath a discussion. As a result, the team is left to sift through the data and rational arguments and wonder why the leader does not address unconstructive behaviour patterns or rein in dominant voices that perpetually speak over people who think differently. At this level, conversations are functional and informational, but they are unlikely to be highly innovative or able to accomplish much other than incremental improvement to the status quo.

**Impactful**

At this level, the Conversation Leader is competent at creating impactful conversations. They are like a conductor able to draw the best from each part of the orchestra to create a harmonious and moving outcome that reflects the musical score. The conductor can hear when the trombones are too loud, the second violin needs to retune, or when the music played is different from the score. Those new notes are deemed errors, and the conductor's guiding focus is to have the orchestra play the music as it is written.

Similarly, the Conversation Leader listens and reflects individual participants' ideas and contributions and notices when someone has fallen silent or is struggling to express themselves. While guiding participants through the agenda items, the Conversation Leader listens for recurring motifs or themes. The leader is very much still driven by the agenda. If unexpected issues or clashes occur, there can be a tendency to rein the group back to the original plan rather than adjusting the course.

Participants experience being respected and heard. There is psychological safety in this space, and, for the most part, they trust the competency of the Conversation Leader. As a result, the team feels uplifted and that they are in it together.

**Indispensable**

At this level, the Conversation Leader moves beyond conducting musicians performing a musical score into leading a jazz band. This form of music allows the group and individual soloists to use frameworks of chord progression, melodic licks, rhythm and improvisation skills to go beyond just reading sheet music. Whereas classical music is composer-driven, jazz is performer-driven. Each performer gets a moment to shine during their solo. You could watch a jazz performance every night for a week, and each time, the sax or bass solo may sound quite different as the individual player has the scope to express themselves musically, within the unifying frame of the song.

This Conversation Leader confidently adapts and responds to what the group needs in any given moment, regardless of the planned agenda. They feel confident to improvise and empower individual contributors because they value the opportunity to learn from new ideas rather than feeling threatened by them. At this level, the Conversation Leader has much deeper expertise and confidence to read subtle cues and group dynamics. They can name and share themes, patterns and disconnections that may emerge during the conversation.

The team experiences a shift that allows it to operate outside the box of "here's how we do things" and incremental change. Team meetings shift from being a "must do" obligation to a "want to do" – an indispensable part of how the team functions. The foundation is set for the group to do innovative, creative and impactful work together consistently.

## Take Action

### ✓ What Works for You?

_____

_____

_____

Think of a meeting you attended that was indispensable – one where you gained clarity by participating and left feeling inspired and part of a team.

What helped create this experience? What choices did the Conversation Leader make that contributed to this experience? Note at least three attributes of that meeting.

_____

_____

_____

### ✓ Where Are You Now, and Where Do You Want to Be?

Review Table 2, which shows the impact of leading Conversations that Count. Answer the following questions:

Where would you place yourself now and why?

_____

_____

_____

Where do you want to be?

_____
_____
_____

Why is that important to you? Why does it matter to your team?

_____
_____
_____

What is possible if you become more adept at leading Conversations that Count?

- What could you realize for yourself, personally and professionally?
- What could be realized for your team and your organization?
- What could the potential impact be for your clients? Your community?

_____
_____
_____
_____
_____

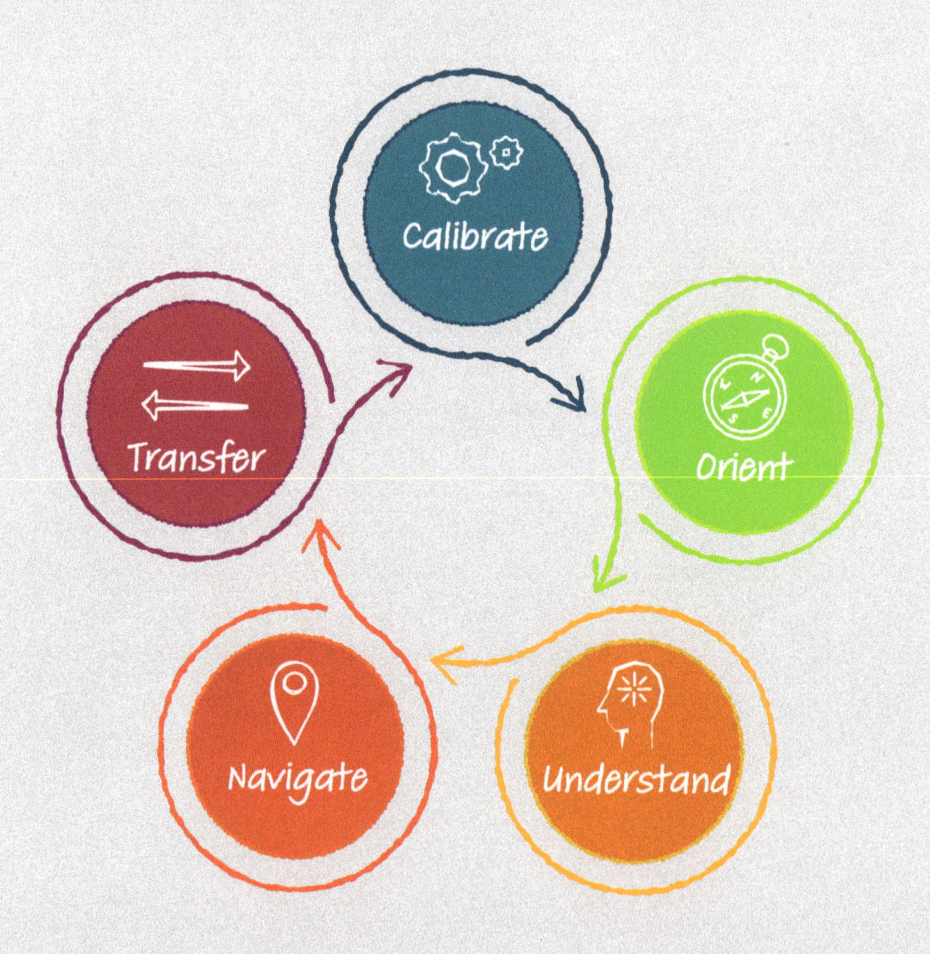

- Calibrate
- Orient
- Understand
- Navigate
- Transfer

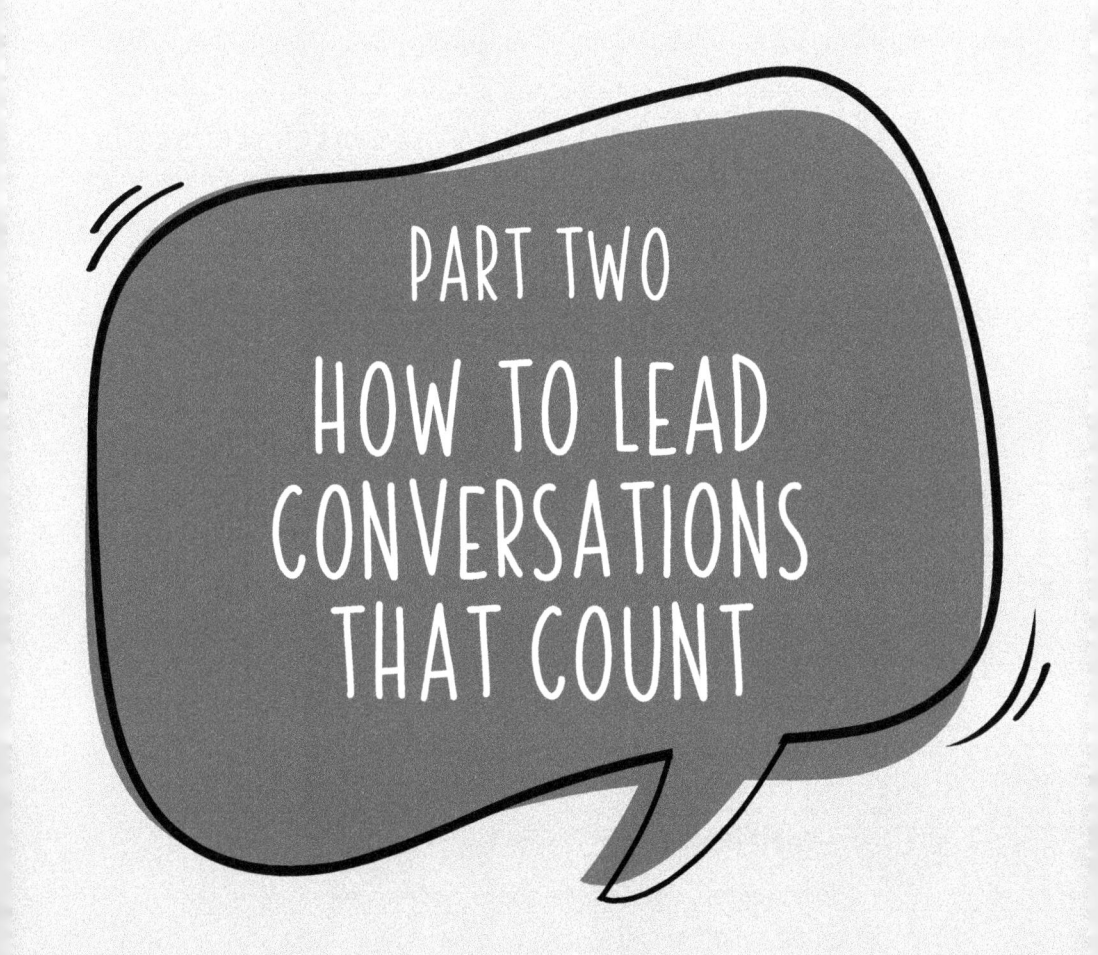

## PART TWO
## HOW TO LEAD CONVERSATIONS THAT COUNT

In this section, you'll learn the essential ingredients to make your next meeting an opportunity to strengthen and deepen your team's relationships and trust. We will focus on five building blocks.

### Calibrate

You'll learn how to do the necessary internal and personal preparation before the meeting starts. Once you've set your intention and are properly calibrated and ready, you're able to be clear, present, and able to reposition when you notice yourself getting off track. The calibrate stage helps you leave behind any baggage you may be carrying from other parts of your day, work, or life so you can be fully present with your team.

### Orient

You'll learn the importance of stepping into your participants' shoes and creating an intention of what you want them to experience from the conversation. You orient yourself to the quality of relationships in your team, knowing that team performance can only be enhanced by a strong level of trust and collaboration. You'll learn how to design your conversation with the end in mind and create the space – physical, virtual, or psychological – for people to do their best work together.

### Understand

In this step, you'll learn about how important it is to truly listen to others, the basics of effective communication and tips for managing group dynamics. These skills are foundational, and yet too often, we haven't experienced them ourselves or lack great role models in how to do this well.

### Navigate

When inevitable differences of opinion and outright conflict arise in meetings, it can be tricky not to take things personally. This step will explain four toxins that can derail a team and how to handle them. You'll also learn how to get to the root cause of conflict, rather than just reacting to the symptoms that may erupt in a discussion.

### Transfer

The work isn't done when the meeting is over. In fact, some of it will now begin in earnest. This final step is about the importance of putting in place the time, structures, and agreements to take the momentum from the meeting into action.

There are bonus points for those of you who have noticed that the word COUNT (as in Conversations that Count) is an acronym for each of the building blocks!

Part Two is like a recipe book. It includes the basic ingredients, but you can decide which dish to create. (Although I highly recommend Calibrate as the opening course at every meeting.)

Each chapter ends with a recipe card, which serves as a high-level summary of the key ideas. When you use the recommended ingredients, you'll be in great shape to have an impactful conversation. I've also noted ingredients that can spoil the dish if used too much or in the wrong proportion. There's room to customize it to meet your needs and communication style. It is also a way to tailor those ideas to your preferences, communication style, and work needs.

Let's dive right in.

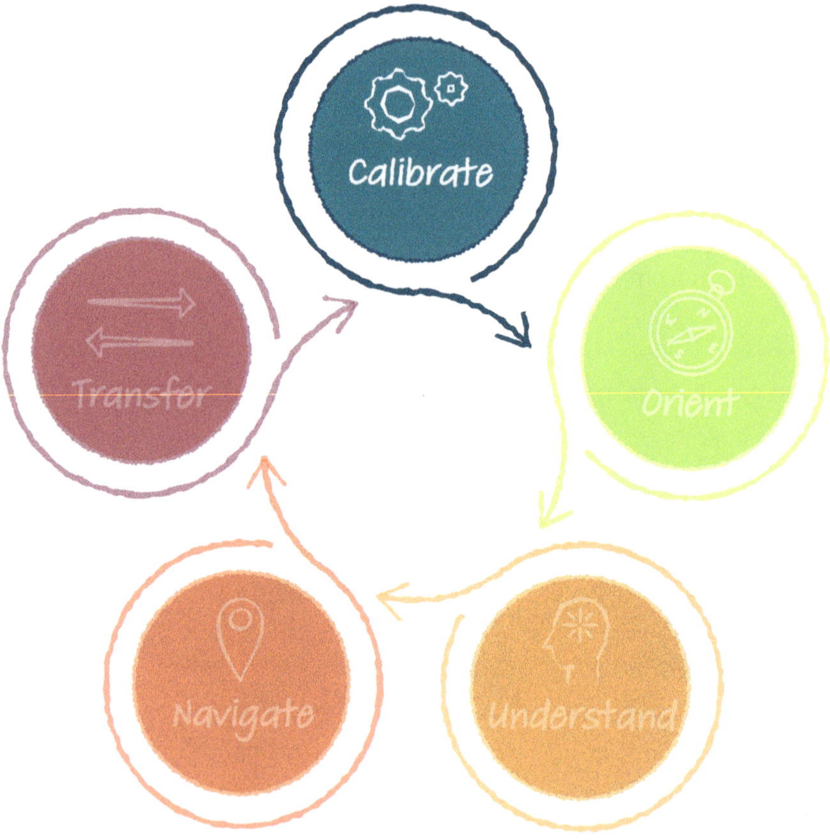
Calibrate
Orient
Understand
Navigate
Transfer

# CHAPTER THREE

# Calibrate

*You can't control the waves,
but you can learn to surf.*

*– Jon Kabat-Zinn*

**Surf's Up!**

During the early days of the pandemic, when my hometown was in full lockdown, taking my dog for a long walk along the shores of Lake Ontario was a sanity-saving necessity. One particularly windy and snowy day, I saw about a dozen surfers braving the frigid waters. Astonished, I was comforted to see they were in full wetsuits and safety gear. As much as I feared they would be tossed about like helpless corks and succumb to hypothermia – they weren't. Despite the sub-zero temperatures, the snow driving into their faces, and the grey skies and icy shores surrounding them, they looked like they were having the time of their lives.

One particular surfer caught my eye. He paddled out on his board, cutting through the oncoming waves, to the spot where he'd chosen to wait for the Big One he was looking to ride to shore. Waves broke continuously over him, but he shook them off and continued to paddle forward. Arriving at his spot, he used his arms to hover and maintain his position. He was patient, checking over his shoulder to decide whether the next swell would be the right one. He clearly had confidence – even just to be in the lake during this winter storm!

Suddenly, a large wave rose behind him, and the moment came to act. In a split second, he jumped to his feet and took a low crouch position. Arms spread, balance distributed on his board, the wave lifted the surfer and his board as it began to crest. He was up, riding the wave – and then he lost his balance and was tossed unceremoniously into the frigid grey lake. Undaunted, he swam over to his board and headed back out to catch his next wave.

Watching this unfolding scene of sanity-challenging bravery, I thought of the many ways that surfers are a blueprint for leading meetings that create Conversations that Count.

## To Calibrate Or Not, That Is the Question

The surfer was a demonstration of calibration in real-time. He was prepared on many levels. First, he had *the right equipment* – surfboard, wet suit, life vest, and buddies on the water, so he wasn't surfing alone. Second, he clearly had *the right experience* – knowing how to read the waves and the wind, picking the best spot to launch based on his knowledge of this particular bay on this specific day.

The third ingredient he demonstrated was *an ability to calibrate*. The verb "calibrate" derives from the noun "caliber". It means the quality of someone's character or the level of their ability and the standard reached. When you calibrate something, you assess its caliber and measure or adjust precisely for a particular function (Merriam-Webster, n.d.).

For each wave, the surfer was attuned to the needs of the moment. Whether waiting for the next wave or shifting his weight on the board to compensate for a stronger-than-expected surge, he was ready to meet the moment. With strength, stamina, patience and trust, the surfer calibrated to the shifting conditions of his surroundings and his energy reserves, and all while keeping his eye on the big goal – a fun, exhilarating ride into shore. The surfer's ability to bring all three of the elements together – equipment, experience, calibration to the waves – allowed him to ride his board all the way to shore.

When leading Conversations that Count, you need to be fully calibrated to the group and the purpose of your meeting. The first area that needs attention is your inner landscape. It takes a certain level of self-awareness and humility to pause and assess your internal thoughts, feelings and beliefs. It involves shifting or setting them aside so they don't become a barrier to being fully present and effective with the people in your conversation.

When Conversation Leaders are not calibrated and tuned in to their own agendas, perspectives and biases, chances are high they will inadvertently throw a meeting off course, undermine psychological safety, and miss the opportunity to get the best from their people. Your ability to pick up some of the nuances and signals from your group and the ever-changing dynamics that are a normal part of group discussion is compromised. As Rebecca Knight wrote in an HBR article, "In every conversation at work, there's the explicit discussion happening – the words being spoken out loud – and the tacit one. To be successful in most organizations, it's important to understand the underlying conversations and reactions that people in the room are having." (Knight, 2018).

If you've ever played a musical instrument, you know how important it is to be in tune. Temperature changes, the amount of use (or disuse), where you place your hands on the strings, and even individual playing style can impact whether the note you play is in tune or not. When you're playing by yourself, it may not be noticeable that your instrument is a bit off-key. But when you get into a group, even with just one other person, being out of tune becomes obvious. It can even be acoustically painful. (This is why I believe parents and teachers of budding violinists deserve some kind of a medal.)

## The Bermuda Triangle of Conversations

Off the southeast coast of the United States, in the Atlantic Ocean, is an area known as the Bermuda Triangle. While not officially recognized by the US Coast Guard or marked on any maps, the legend of the Bermuda Triangle was popularized initially as a place where ships and aircraft mysteriously disappeared, often never to be found again. The myth is that even experienced ship captains or pilots lose their way and face peril there.

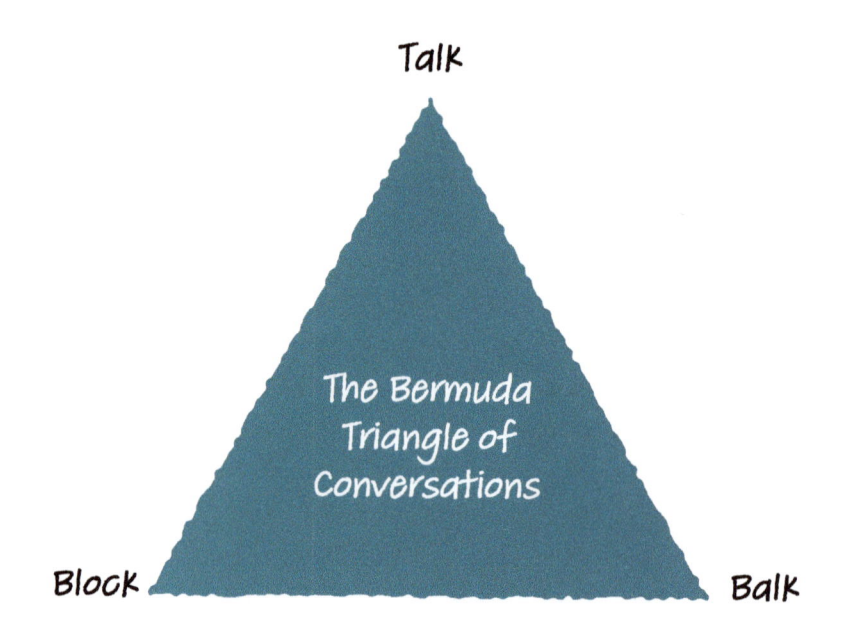

*Figure 3: The Bermuda Triangle of Conversations*

Conversation Leaders can exhibit three behavioural patterns that lead a group into its own Bermuda Triangle. When these behaviours show up, participants are disengaged, disenfranchised and even disgruntled.

**Talk: It's More Dissertation Than Dialogue**

The Conversation Leader is doing most of the talking. Rather than a two-way dialogue, where all participants have the chance to contribute and speak, the direction of discussion is primarily one-way, with the leader taking up the air time.

My children and I have a running joke when we watch movies together, and a character starts monologuing. Invariably the person is so busy expounding their point of view, they miss important clues around them and end up suffering some kind of consequence. Whether it's not noticing the open manhole cover in the street or failing to see someone hiding behind the curtain in a darkened room, the monologuer pays a price for their inattention.

From the participant's perspective, it feels like being talked at instead of spoken with. This style of engagement is more of the "sage on the stage" rather than a "guide on the side". Participants may wonder why they bothered to show up to the meeting if they have no chance to provide input.

At in-person gatherings, this style of conversational leadership feels more like a lecture or presentation than a discussion. The dynamic is amplified in virtual settings, where people's attention is easily distracted by the effortless ability to click open a new browser, surreptitiously scan their email in-box while looking engaged, or even turn off their cameras altogether.

## Block: Leader as Judge and Jury of Discussion

Another signal that the Conversation Leader isn't fully calibrated with the group dynamics is that they block the evolution of the discussion. Instead of helping to draw out the group's ideas and understanding, the Conversation Leader actively judges everything according to criteria that are often not shared with the group. You might hear a blocking leader say, "That's not what we're here to discuss," or "I don't think that's a good idea," or "We've been over this already, let's move on". This dynamic can lead to the group feeling unwilling and even unsafe to participate. As we saw in the earlier story, shutting Sandra down when she had an idea that didn't fit with Tom's pre-determined criteria led the entire group to stop participating.

When a leader demonstrates blocking behaviour, try pointing out the block by asking questions or redirecting back to the stated purpose of the meeting and renegotiating as a group how to get the collective work done. Participants may have sidebar conversations in a break to problem-solve issues or negotiate some kind of truce to get the meeting back on track.

In a virtual meeting, impromptu conversations to touch base with each other are limited. While online participants can chat privately with one another, it's difficult for a group to find its alignment and common purpose if the Conversation Leader is continually blocking the group. With virtual meetings often held with compressed agendas to avoid too much "Zoom fatigue," it requires courage and trust to call for a spontaneous break so participants and the Conversation Leader can step back for a few moments to regroup.

## Balk: It's My Way or the Highway

One of the more extreme signals of being out of sync with the group is when a leader balks at certain points in the discussion. When a horse balks in the jumping ring, it suddenly and stubbornly refuses to leap over the obstacle in front of it, often tossing its rider in the process. In a conversation, balking is reacting, rather than responding, to the issues raised.

This reaction can manifest as cutting the meeting short, refusing to discuss certain issues, or asserting power or privilege to shut the contributions of others down. You might hear, "You're new to this organization, and that's an issue above your pay grade," or "New hires aren't supposed to be doing that".

At in-person meetings, it is easier to read body language and pick up the subtle signals that the discussion is heading into difficult territory. Those cues are harder to discern when groups are working online. When a Conversation Leader engages in balking behaviour or tactics in a virtual meeting, it can feel like it comes out of the blue. This break in the flow can feel quite abrupt, and the Conversation Leader will have to work hard to rebuild and regain trust and cooperation from the group.

## You Set the Bar

Why is the step of calibration so important? Consider the act of calibrating yourself before you start your meeting as the equivalent of stretching your muscles before you run a sprint. If you don't do it, chances are you'll walk into your conversation carrying a whole lot of baggage from previous experiences and perspectives. You're starting the conversation weighed down with:

- Beliefs
- Biases
- Unprocessed issues from previous discussions
- Pressure and stress you feel to perform and deliver to people you report to, who are likely not even in the meeting

- Judgments about people you'll be talking with
- Frustrations carried from unrelated incidents that impact your state and are easily picked up by others. It might be your feelings about the person who cut you off on the highway or someone who hasn't yet responded to an email.
- Worries range from specific (Will my internet connection be reliable today when it wasn't last week?) to global and existential (Will we ever get back to normal after this pandemic? or How will global warming impact my loved ones?).

Inner self-talk also impacts our ability to be present and resilient and show up confidently as our best in any situation. Recent research from Queen's University in 2020 shows that the average person has 6,200 thoughts per day (Berman, 2020). A majority of those thoughts tend to be negative, as human brains have a "negativity bias", which evolved as a survival mechanism that constantly scans our environment for threats (Hanson, et al., 2009).

If left unattended, negative self-talk can impact mental health, motivation and the ability to recognize and act on opportunities. Elizabeth Scott writes that this stress is primarily "due to the fact that their reality is altered to create an experience where they don't have the ability to reach the goals they've set for themselves." (Scott, 2020).

Phew! That's a lot to have on your plate, and you haven't even got to the meeting yet!

Let's go back to our surfer out on his board riding a wave. Imagine he's worrying whether his contract will be renewed or reliving an argument with a roommate about whose turn it was to clean the kitchen. With that level of inner distraction, it would be hard to stay alert, agile and present to the conditions and be able to ride that wave into shore without getting tossed back into the lake.

> The success of an intervention depends on the interior condition of the intervenor.
>
> – Bill O'Brien

The problems organizations now face are challenging. When experiencing rapid change, low or declining engagement rates, and rising uncertainty, we all need our best thinking caps on. Collectively, humanity is facing some existential crises – environmental, political, socio-economic – that will require innovation, agility and resilience to solve.

Old roles, strategies and reporting structures may be obsolete.

But the heart of solving any kind of challenge – whether it's global warming, restructuring a business to thrive in a pandemic, or changing the onboarding of new hires – lies in the quality of our relationships. How do we listen to one another? Do we learn from one another? Can we explore common ground to amplify strengths and build bridges where there may be gaps or differences of opinions?

## Calibration Strategies

The first person you must learn to lead is yourself. Taking time to calibrate yourself to lead the conversation ensures you have prepared your awareness and perspectives, not just your agenda and PowerPoint deck. The key components of the Calibrate stage are Mindset, Motor and Model, as outlined in Figure 4.

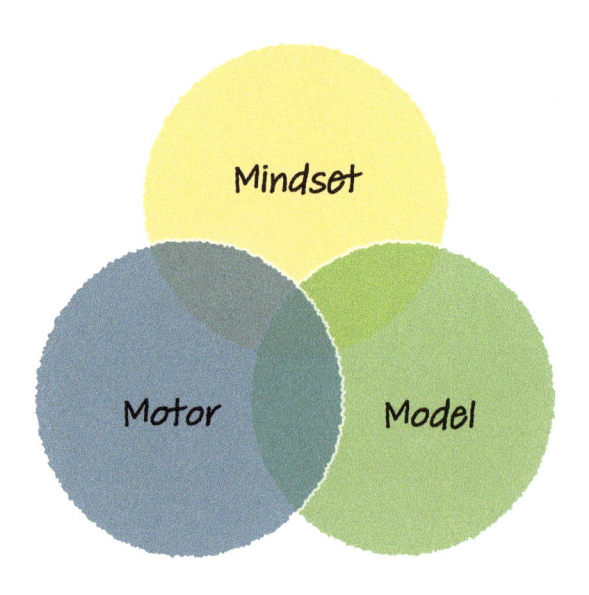

*Figure 4: Calibration Strategies*

## Mindset: Curiosity and An Open Mind Will Take You Far

Without an open mind, you'll miss lots of valuable information. You don't know what you don't know. Nothing shuts down contributions and engagement faster than the meeting leader with a fixed opinion and people feeling their input is falling on deaf ears.

When operating under stress or feeling the pressure to perform in leading the conversation, it can be tempting to assert your knowledge, experience and desires as the way to go. Relying on what you already know and staying in your comfort zone is one way to manage the pressure and uncertainty. Yet adopting a beginner's mindset and being open to discovering what you don't know, that you don't know, is crucial. Stay humble and appreciate the wisdom in the room.

One of my clients, Nina (not her real name), was a rising executive who was very successful at her work, yet she tended to be a perfectionist. Nina's attention to detail and her ability to think and plan strategically set her up for a series of promotions in a relatively short time. But as her responsibilities and scope of work increased, she struggled to cope with unexpected challenges or the time frames required to carry projects across the finish line. Nina battled with Imposter Syndrome, and her mindset interpreted setbacks, even minor ones, as signs that she was not as capable as her career trajectory would suggest. At some deep level, she believed the universe was out to punish her for not being good enough.

In one of our coaching sessions, we took a deep dive into this mindset. Nina recognized its origins in a childhood that saw her attend many different schools as her parents were posted to different military locations. Growing up, as soon as she felt comfortable and accepted by one particular group of friends, the family would move, and Nina had to get used to a new school environment and social circle yet again. For Nina, the rising professional woman, this mindset was becoming a roadblock.

"What if the universe is out to polish, not punish you when these setbacks arise?" I asked her. "What's possible if you adopt that mindset, even temporarily?" Nina fell silent, her eyes downcast for a moment, and then she looked up with a radiant smile and a look of relief. "Yes, I have developed a whole raft of skills and experience that help me to overcome setbacks and unexpected things pretty quickly!"

In a later coaching session, Nina reaffirmed that this mindset shift had been profound. Instead of experiencing setbacks as a personal indictment of her ability, she saw it as an opportunity to sharpen and strengthen her decision-making and execution skills. She said. "What's been a bonus is that I've been able to share this shift in perspective with my team as well. Instead of saying "Oh no!" when something goes wrong, we say "Oh, interesting!" and get curious. We are all feeling much more resilient and undaunted when we hit a glitch of any kind."

> Don't think about why you question, simply don't stop questioning. Don't worry about what you can't answer, and don't try to explain what you can't know. Curiosity is its own reason. Aren't you in awe when you contemplate the mysteries of eternity, of life, of the marvellous structure behind reality?
>
> And this is the miracle of the human mind – to use its constructions, concepts and formulas as tools to explain what man sees, feels and touches. Try to comprehend a little more each day. Have holy curiosity.
>
> – *Albert Einstein*

Unlock your curiosity by asking open-ended questions. Here are a few powerful ones to start with:

- "What if....?"
- "What is the potential gift in this situation for me? For my group?"
- "What is the real challenge here now?"
- "What could be in my blind spot that I just can't see right now?"
- "What is it I/we want?"
- "I wonder...."

## Motor: You are the Engine that Drives the Process

At one point in my career, I was the Director of Development at a renowned independent school in Toronto. I had three young children and was in the process of a divorce, and we had just launched a major capital campaign at work. There was a lot on my plate, yet I felt I was juggling everything fairly well.

One day driving to work, I noticed the fuel light was on. "Ah, I can fill up the tank later," I thought. But as I approached my office, my car started to sputter. I pressed the gas, but the engine wasn't getting any more power. With a growing sense of anxiety, I recalled that the light had been on the day before – and the day before that too. In my zeal to juggle all the balls I had in the air, I had neglected the basics of filling up my gas tank. Thankfully, I managed to reach the parking lot, where my car coasted to a spot, and I could safely call for assistance. That day I realized the truth of the adage "you can't run on fumes" – both literally and metaphorically.

As the Conversation Leader, you are the engine that drives the whole process of the meeting. Your energy and presence create the ecosystem for you and your group to do the work. If your tank is empty, you aren't going anywhere, and neither are your participants.

Part of your meeting preparation is to ensure you are ready to show up fully for your group. What do you need to do to ensure you can show up at your meeting prepared and focused on what you need to accomplish?

Here are some tips to keep your engine running at peak effectiveness:

- Ensure your physical needs are met – be well-rested and well-nourished

- Be organized for your conversation – make sure you have what you need to be successful in terms of materials, location, briefing
- Ask for any assistance you need from others to be ready to "surf" in the meeting
- Check your blind spots by reflecting on any baggage from previous conversations, issues or people that may offer any level of doubt or discomfort. Noticing and naming issues in advance helps to give you some perspective about them, rather than letting yourself become reactive to them in the meeting.

Calibration is like making sure your windshield is clean. Even a smear or large dead bug blocks your view of what's ahead or makes you have to work harder to see around that obstacle of vision. Cleaning dust, debris or snow from your car isn't something you do once. It's part of routine maintenance that enables you to see clearly and drive safely.

It takes personal preparation to be in the right state for leading effective conversations. Create a clear intention, notice any potential blocks or biases that may be clouding your awareness, and do what's needed so you can be fully present.

## To tame it, you need to name it.

### Model: People Do What You Do, Not What You Say

As the Conversation Leader, you set the bar. Your presence creates an ecosystem for participants to work together. If you've been a parent, you already know that children will do as you do and not as you say. As a role model for listening, acknowledging, contributing, and questioning, participants will follow your lead, so be mindful of the example you set.

Children are the best teachers for parents when it comes to setting a role model. I was called into nursery school because my youngest son, at the tender age of four, was apparently teaching his classmates how to curse like a sailor. Embarrassed, I meekly explained to his teacher that as the youngest of three children, he was likely picking up a few unwanted habits from his older siblings, who were already well into grade school. Yet on the drive home, as I earnestly told my son about the importance of being respectful with our words, another driver cut in front of my car without a signal. In a nanosecond, I yelled out a choice word that would make the late George Carlin proud. I still remember looking in the rear-view mirror and seeing my son's little face. Eyebrow raised, his wry smile said, "Sure, Mom, you were saying something about being respectful with our words? Do continue." I realized my four-year-old was, with a glance, calling me out as a hypocrite, even though he didn't know what that word meant.

In leading conversations, you are constantly setting an example. The question is whether that example contributes to or takes away from creating a Conversation that Counts. From my twenty years of experience coaching individuals, here are a few principles I find most useful:

### *Integrity*

The first person you need to lead is yourself. When you have integrity, you do what you say, and you say what you'll do. If that changes for any reason, you share what and why in a transparent and timely manner. When people know you operate from integrity, they feel they can count on you. You have their back. A leader that exhibits little self-awareness or willingness to manage their state doesn't inspire trust and conviction in those around him/her.

### Humility

You may have a different position on the organizational chart than the people you're having a conversation with, but that alone will not necessarily buy cooperation, collaboration or commitment from others. Being humble and recognizing you too have things to learn from others helps build trust and sets the expectation for learning together. Humility demonstrates your growth mindset and willingness to reflect upon your choices, successes, and failures and learn from them all.

### Willingness

To read the room, you need to be willing to read yourself and recognize where you need to re-calibrate. It also requires a willingness to be vulnerable, which means admitting when you don't know or feel stuck.

While vulnerability can feel risky, it invites people to have greater trust and connection with you. Asking for help creates opportunities for others to contribute their leadership. You also serve as a role model and normalize that it is totally acceptable and safe not to know and ask for what you need.

> Your willingness to be vulnerable can be your greatest strength.

## Tips for Virtual Conversations

The strategies we've discussed here are designed to support you, as the Conversation Leader, to show up prepared, so you can be fully present and ready to go when the meeting starts. If you've done the preparation to calibrate yourself and lead with presence, but your meeting is virtual and your technology is subpar, then you risk the ability to have the best possible connection and impact with your participants.

Well-functioning audio and video equipment isn't a matter of vanity when it comes to video conferencing; they are crucial tools for your professional credibility and impact. Poor lighting, spotty internet, and a sub-optimal camera position can distract your participants and undermine your efforts at leading Conversations that Count.

Here are some of the most important components to get right when it comes to creating an effective home studio for your virtual meetings:

### 💡 Make Effective Eye Contact

Position your computer so that you have good eye contact with your participants. I am still surprised when, at least once a week, I'm in a session where someone's laptop camera is positioned so low that the most prominent view is the inside of their nose! Looking at the camera lens is how you establish eye contact. It helps build a sense of connection and trust with your participants.

If your camera lens is positioned too low, you'll be bending your head down, which sends more of a signal of authority figure to your audience than you may wish. (Remember a time when you were caught having dessert before dinnertime, and how it felt when your parent scolded you?) Body language experts say raising your chin beyond horizontal to look in the camera communicates superiority or arrogance (Parvez, 2015).

When you're talking, it's easy to look at your participants on the screen, but remember as much as possible to look at the camera lens to maintain that eye contact. I keep a sticky note with a smiley face beside my camera lens. If you do use your computer's camera, raise it high enough to look directly into it. You can also consider using external webcams, DSLR cameras and tripods, or other solutions to give you better quality cameras that can adjust to various lighting situations. In their useful book, *Suddenly Virtual: Making Remote Meetings Work*, authors Reed and Allen argue that "high-quality video and audio are a new best practice for effective virtual meetings." (Reed & Allen, 2021).

Eye contact won't make much impact if you aren't visible. Take advantage of natural lighting in your space to ensure that your face is well-lit. Try to position yourself so you aren't directly in front of direct light, where you'll be in shadow. Supplementary lights, such as a simple ring light on a tripod behind the webcam, is a relatively inexpensive and reliable solution that ensures you can be seen, no matter the time of day.

### 💡 Pay Attention to Your Delivery

Pay attention to your energy and how you deliver on camera. You may think your volume is good and you have good liveliness and modulation in your voice, but if you see a recording of yourself, you may be disappointed. If the camera puts on ten pounds, it also seems to suck 20 percent of the life out of us as well as people struggle with feeling self-conscious, and their delivery style becomes more formal and rigid.

One of my pet peeves is a person obviously reading notes on their desk while trying to present. Deliver your point of view and information, don't read it; otherwise, you'll put people to sleep! As far as possible, show up on camera as if you were leading the group in a boardroom or the office. You'd glance at your notes, but likely be more animated and make eye contact with your participants to check in with them. Do the same thing in your virtual meeting. If necessary, stand to dial up your energy and presence.

I love performing in community musical theatre. I've learned from being on stage that creating the intention to connect energetically with the person in the very back row in the balcony section helps bring out everything I have to give in my performance. It enables me to "leave it all on the stage" as my cast members and I tell each other before the curtain rises. I translate that into my virtual meetings, imagining I am reaching through the lens with energy to connect with the people I'm talking with. As part of my preparation before the meeting, I'll take a moment to appreciate who will be attending and feel grateful for the gift of their time and attention they are making by even showing up. Maintaining eye contact and sending energy through the technology builds relationships and connection.

When you are leading virtual meetings, one of the many faces you'll see on screen is your own. Most of us are not fans of this reality, as it distracts from being authentic and powerful in delivery. It's cognitively exhausting to peel your eyes off yourself and dampen the stream of negative inner dialogue that can trigger. "Why is my hair so frizzy when I use conditioner?" or "Oh no, has everyone else also noticed I'm wearing the same shirt as last week's meeting?" To stop yourself from going down that rabbit hole, consult the guide of your selected videoconferencing platform and choose "Hide Self-View".

### 💡 Position Yourself in Frame

If possible, try to ensure your head and shoulders are well-framed with your camera. You want to be close enough that people can see your facial expressions, but not that the top of your head is cut off. Having space at the sides and top of the frame allows you to communicate with gestures. If you're too far away, you'll lose some of the connection you're trying to foster. If you're too close, it doesn't feel natural and can even feel like an invasion of personal space, even though you're working virtually.

### 💡 Be Intentional with Your Background

When working from home, not everyone may have the option of a separate home office with a door. Our home environments may mean working from a dining room table, couch or even a bedroom. You'll be having meetings in a space that may be active with family, pets, roommates or outside sounds. I have some clients who now ask how my dog is, as Kaylee decides to shove a toy in my lap while I'm having a meeting. Working via videoconference means that people get an intimate glimpse into your home environment. While this may feel uncomfortable, it's a significant opportunity to build a level of relatedness and authenticity with your participants.

Be intentional about what the camera shows in your background. Reducing visual clutter or stimuli helps lessen the potential for distraction. Curate it so that what people see helps them understand who you are and what you value. Favourite photos, artwork, books, or even houseplants can do the trick. Sure, put your Star Wars figurine collection in the background if that helps to give a glimpse of you as a whole person, not just a professional colleague.

There are virtual backgrounds available, with some increasing in sophistication and effectiveness. Ultimately the choice about their use comes back to being intentional. Some of my corporate clients have provided virtual backgrounds of the office where people worked together. They are professionally shot and inspire a sense of familiarity and connection for their employees. Sometimes it can be fun to ask people to choose a virtual background that shows where they'd like to travel when the pandemic situation eases. That enables you to learn more about each other and build connection about personal interests. Beware, though, as some virtual backgrounds are cheesy and can become wearying if used constantly. (Also, seeing someone's hand disappear while they take a sip of water is distracting.) Using virtual backgrounds also removes the opportunity to bring someone into your home, which can be a powerful way to build trust and relatability.

### 💡 Find a Virtual Meeting Producer

It's important to consider that you may feel more pressure running a virtual meeting than when you only had to walk into a meeting room. It takes a lot more to manage the discussion and the technology.

If you can, get support with producing the meeting. Find someone who is experienced with the tech and can troubleshoot any issues that participants may encounter. Get someone else to run the polls, set up the breakout rooms, and help keep track of time so you can be fully present and available to lead the discussion and tune into the ever-evolving group dynamics. Even if you are tech-savvy and comfortable with virtual conferencing platforms, be mindful of whether multi-tasking in both leading the discussion and supporting the tech will serve your objectives for the conversation.

## Take Action

### CALIBRATE INGREDIENTS

**More of:**
- ☑ Define your bar — set a personal intention
- ☑ Adapt a mindset of curiosity
- ☑ Fill your tank
- ☑ Decide what you want to role model

**Add Your Own Ingredients:**
_____
_____

**Less of:**
- ☒ Stuck in the Bermuda Triangle — Talk-Block-Balk
- ☒ Persistent inner dialogue
- ☒ Act as judge and jury
- ☒ Self-doubt and self-scrutiny
- ☒ Performance anxiety

**Watch Out For:**
_____
_____

### ✓ Your Personal Intention

What's your personal intention for the next conversation you're going to lead? Keep it simple. It may be to stay curious or to speak less and listen more.

**My personal intention is:** _____

_____

_____

Think of a way to remember your intention during the meeting. Perhaps write it on a sticky note, placed next to your computer or share it with another person – or even out loud with the group at the start of your conversation.

**I will remember this intention by:** _____

_____

_____

### ✅ Clean Your Windshield

Take time to prepare yourself internally for the conversation. What thoughts, beliefs or fears might get in the way of being present and operating at full capacity? Take some deep breaths, and ask your inner wisdom what you need to let go of so you can have a clear view of your group's dynamics and lead a Conversation that Counts. Write down what might get in the way:

_____

_____

_____

_____

Having brought awareness to what might get in the way, what can you do now to let them go? You may wish to take some deep conscious breaths or meditate. Imagine packaging those issues up in a balloon and letting them float away for now. Take some intentional action to set those issues that may be a distraction for you to the side for now.

_____

_____

_____

_____

### ✅ Create a Recalibration Protocol

If you notice you are losing your balance in the meeting and feel you're about to get tossed off your surfboard, what can you do immediately to recalibrate? It can be something simple, like taking three deep breaths when you feel off-center. Call for a pause. Recommit to your intention. Make a plan right now for how to get back on your board when you get knocked into the water.

_____

_____

_____

_____

### ✅ Calibrate Your Home Studio

Set up a virtual meeting with yourself and assess the basic elements of your home office/studio. Ensure your camera, lighting, framing and background support you in being seen, heard, felt and understood when you lead your next virtual meeting.

Things to do to improve my home studio:

_____

_____

_____

_____

_____

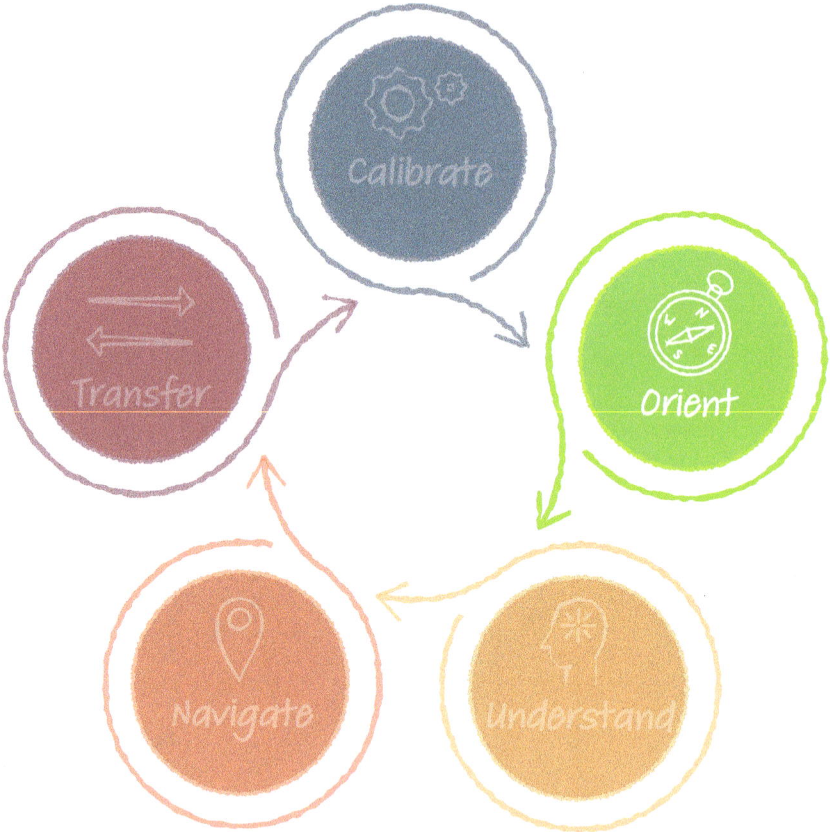

Calibrate
Orient
Understand
Navigate
Transfer

# CHAPTER FOUR

# Orient

*The greatest tragedy for any human being is going through their entire lives believing the only perspective that matters is their own.*

– *Doug Baldwin*

**Has Anyone Got a Mic?**

As soon as I walked into the large, cavernous ballroom, I knew there would be challenges. I was working with a client who was doing a two-day community consultation with about forty members from various remote, small First Nations communities to plan for a new vision of social service delivery. The participants were members of Indigenous communities that faced heart-breaking challenges every day. High rates of suicide, a litany of health challenges from poor drinking water, lack of adequate housing, and a long legacy of government policies had marginalized and undermined Indigenous autonomy for decades. They compounded the ongoing social, economic, and mental health challenges that formed the context for discussing a new social service delivery model.

This two-day discussion, run by an external facilitator from within the Indigenous communities, required deep listening, psychological safety, and ample opportunity to allow people's voices to be heard as they designed a future social service plan for their communities. My role was as the graphic recorder, visually capturing the key points and learnings of the group discussion.

As I gazed up at the enormous hotel ballroom ceiling, I saw a significant mismatch between the ornate physical space and the vulnerable, intimate and deep conversations I'd anticipated would part of the consultation session. I was immediately concerned about acoustics. Seating for the participants required only about 30 percent of the ballroom space, and the tables were gathered in one section. The only apparent audio in the room was a single microphone atop a formal wooden podium set in one corner. The cavernous space would swallow up even a big, booming voice.

I warned the client that acoustics might be problematic and recommended we secure additional microphones before the retreat began. The session facilitator, however, confidently assured the client that they would not need mics. In fact, she asserted, it would be good practice for the participants to learn to speak up to be heard. The client deferred to their facilitator, and the meeting began.

As the session unfolded, it became apparent that the room wasn't conducive to deep conversations about difficult issues. The lighting was dim, and it was hard to hear across the large tables, let alone anywhere else. Most participants sat back in their chairs, listening to the facilitator and the client speaking as loudly as possible at the front of the room. The participants appeared either unimpressed or uncertain about how to proceed. As most of the morning session was in PowerPoint presentations, participant engagement and contribution were minimal.

By the morning break, the facilitator was feeling quite confronted. "They just aren't speaking up for themselves," she declared. I stepped forward to offer that there could be other reasons for the silence. "With all due respect, most of the morning session has been presentations from the front of the room. There has been little opportunity for them to actively engage in discussion. Also, the acoustics in this room are bad. People are spending their attention trying to listen to what's being said, and it's not easy. The space of this room is siphoning off the group energy. With additional microphones, people wouldn't have to work so hard, and they would feel more connected to the discussion because they could hear clearly."

The client agreed. Before we reconvened, the hotel provided a few handheld microphones for the participants and the facilitator. With proper acoustics now established, the change in the group dynamic was remarkable. The group leaned forward to listen. They contributed to the conversation, and their voices were heard.

## Avoiding Meeting Frustration

Have you ever left a meeting more confused and frustrated than when you started? One where the conversation was stilted, contrived or superficial, instead of engaging and participatory? Or where the work you expected to do wasn't possible because the meeting space didn't accommodate your group size or needs? These meetings end in frustration because the needs of the participants weren't seen as the important starting point. Meetings held as obligations to knock items off your to-do list, miss the opportunity to create memorable experiences and shared meaning about what's important in your work together.

Sadly, this kind of experience is far too common. Let's be honest – even before the pandemic struck, meetings left much to be desired. As you read in the ballroom story, the basic physical elements of the meeting room – its excessive size and poor acoustics – had a radical impact on the group's ability to engage and connect, slowing their progress in meeting the objectives that had been established.

In this chapter, we'll focus on Orient – the second step of creating Conversations that Count. This stage is about articulating the experience and impact you want to have on your team's relationships and connections. You will always need to focus on objectives and goals, but at the Orient stage, we're talking about putting yourself in the shoes of your participants. Imagine what is important for them to receive from their investment of time and energy in your meeting.

> *Success is a journey, not a destination. The doing is often more important than the outcome.*
>
> *– Arthur Ashe*

## The Cost of Meaningless Meetings

It has never been more challenging to lead and manage teams in business. The pace of change is relentless, and everyone is expected to do more with less. Staying competitive and relevant in the marketplace requires you to get the best from your people. Creative thinking, deep commitment, and a willingness to go the extra mile to find solutions that work are critical to success.

The organization, Better Meetings, surveyed workers throughout the United States and found the following interesting statistics.

- Seventy-eight percent of people feel their meeting schedule is either always or sometimes, out of control, with most blaming their crazy meeting schedules on upper management (38 percent) or their direct manager (16 percent)
- Twenty-one percent of workers say the single biggest thing that would help them do more with less is having fewer meetings to get through the week
- Workers say 10 percent of their week is taken up by useful or productive meetings, while almost the same amount (8 percent) is made up of wasteful meetings
- The five main meeting problems were identified as lack of participant preparation (28 percent), poor communication (20 percent), time allocated is not observed (17 percent), no follow-up on tasks (25 percent) and no minutes (13 percent)
- For the average length of meetings, 49 percent were between 30-60 minutes; 37 percent were 1–2 hours, 7 percent were less than 30 minutes, and another 7 percent were over 2 hours (Martin, 2020).

In a 2017 Harvard Business Review article, *Stop the Meeting Madness*, Perlow, Hadley and Eun revealed that, on average, executives are caught in meetings for up to 23 hours per week. Of 182 senior managers surveyed, 65 percent say meetings stop them from finishing individual work, and 71 percent consider meetings unproductive and inefficient; 64 percent said meetings come at the expense of deep thinking; 62 percent said meetings miss opportunities to bring the team closer together. When wasteful meetings occur, workers often lose valuable time needed to complete tasks and need to stay late or take time out of their weekends to do so.

Companies pay the price for poorly run meetings. A study of twenty organizations showed that dysfunctional meeting behaviours (including wandering off-topic, complaining and criticizing) were associated with lower levels of market share, innovation and employment stability.

Rethinking approaches to meetings showed employees perceived significant improvements in team collaboration (42 percent increase), psychological safety to speak up and express opinions (a 32 percent increase), and team performance (a 28 percent increase). Satisfaction with work/life balance increased from 62 to 92 percent (Perlow, et al., 2017).

## Begin with the End in Mind

The stakes of getting conversations right have never been more important. We need to solve complex issues, and the quality of our relationships and ability to speak with one another is crucial. Two key problems present obstacles to getting the best out of people in your conversation: engagement and change fatigue.

### Engaging Your People

Employee engagement surveys paint a dismal picture. Gallup does annual surveys of employee engagement in the United States, and year-on-year, it shows that only 30 percent of employees are actively engaged at work. The remaining 70 percent of American employees are either disengaged or actively disengaged at work (Gallup, 2020).

A lack of strong engagement impacts every key performance indicator you care to measure. Productivity, profitability and customer satisfaction soar, while employee turnover, absenteeism, and workplace safety issues decline when people care about their work and feel engaged. Gallup estimates the cost of disengagement is anywhere from $450-550 billion annually in the USA and includes the cost of lost productivity and employee churn and resulting damage to workplace culture (Wong, 2019).

People leave managers, not companies, confirming that managers and leaders are the most significant factors influencing employee engagement. Gallup's survey also shows that only 35 percent of managers are engaged at work, which is difficult because they account for at least 70 percent of the variance in employee engagement. When there is regular and meaningful communication with the manager, employees are three times more likely to be engaged (Gallup, 2020).

Another huge influence is generational differences in the workplace. For the first time, there are now five generations working together – from Traditionalists born 1925 to 1945, through to millennials and Generation Z (Purdue University Global, n.d.). Millennials – born between 1981 and 2000 – are expected to make up 75 percent of the global workforce by 2025. Yet only 28 percent feel their current organization is making full use of their skills (Deloitte, 2016). Each generation of workers brings a different set of expectations, communication styles, defining values and motivation.

The rise of the gig economy is yet another factor that influences who is in your conversation. Not everyone will be a full-time employee of your organization. The labour pool is changing with more employers tapping into using workers from the gig economy, independent contractors, and part-time staff.

Conversations with your team are not just an opportunity to help work get done. They form and strengthen relationships across varied groups that will sustain and inspire them to bring their best to the job at hand.

**Change Fatigue**

Every organization is undergoing change, yet the success rate of major change initiatives is only 54 percent, according to a 2103 Strategy& Katzenbach Center Survey (Strategy&, 2013). According to its survey of global senior executives on culture and change management, three major obstacles account for a 48 percent failure rate of major change initiatives:

1. Change fatigue: The exhaustion, cynicism, and pressure on staff from poorly planned or rushed change initiatives or being asked to make too many changes at once.
2. Lack of capabilities: To keep change sustainable over time, companies need to ensure that skills, process design, and operational structures can support it.
3. Lack of frontline ownership: When key change issues are determined in the C-suite with little input from those who need to execute the decisions, the need for an agreement for change can limit your success.

Endless meetings, death by PowerPoint, stressed-out workers operating in silos, and the continuous request of workers to accomplish more with fewer resources are the environment in which most work occurs. Thanks to the COVID-19 pandemic, we can add the stress of constantly adapting to the challenges of living and working in a global pandemic and Zoom fatigue as issues that get in the way of full engagement and participation. Is it any wonder that it's hard to get people on the same page?

## Orient Ingredients

To create a Conversation that Counts, you need to think like an architect designing a specific space for the occupants. The best architect puts themselves in their shoes and imagines the kind of environment that will best support their client's desired lifestyle, aesthetics, and need for function. Whether you are meeting face-to-face or virtually, what kind of environment space do you want to create. What will achieve the best outcome? Think about three key components: Purpose, Plan and Parts.

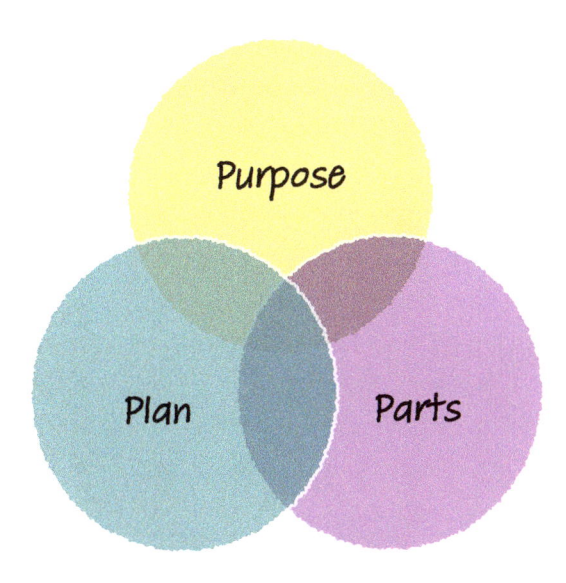

*Figure 5: Orient Strategies*

**Purpose: Purpose Provides Perspective**

What is the bigger context for the discussion? How is what you're talking about relevant and necessary now? It's important to anchor the purpose of the conversation in some context. With only 20 percent of employees reporting that they feel actively engaged in their work, talking at them longer won't help.

Stating a clear purpose – the Why – helps the group keep its eyes on the prize. Priya Parker, the author of *The Art of Gathering*, argues that without committing to a "bold, sharp purpose, we often let old or faulty assumptions about why we gather dictate the form of our gatherings. We end up gathering in ways that don't serve us or not connecting when we ought to." (Parker, 2018).

When I worked as a senior policy advisor at the provincial government, I was involved in a massive initiative to re-examine and re-align the system of provincial-municipal transfers for all social service programs. The scope was large, the issues were complex, and multiple stakeholders and community members needed to be consulted. The general purpose of the initiative was relatively clear and agreed – to make sure the right level of government was paying for programs that supported people in the community. But that clear focus often didn't transfer into the meetings. I remember feeling bleary-eyed and as though my head was filled with sawdust when meetings would ping-pong seemingly randomly between fact-finding, lobbying and issues that didn't apply to 90 percent of the people in the room. They would get lost in explanations of antiquated legislative and regulatory frameworks and developing potential communications strategies for a policy shift that wasn't yet fully formulated. All this often in one meeting!

Articulating a defined and compelling meeting purpose allows participants to understand its relevance, prioritize the conversation subject in terms of their attention and preparation for the discussion, and foster alignment to the ultimate desired outcomes. There may be some in your conversation, perhaps those who are new to the organization, who aren't fully aware of the bigger context of the organization's mission or values. Don't assume that everyone understands or is on board with the purpose.

> *People don't buy what you do;*
> *they buy why you do it.*
>
> *– Simon Sinek*

Conversations will not always go smoothly. A shared sense of purpose and connection to the bigger purpose and its impact on clients, communities, or the organization's mission can provide the motivation, perspective, and trust needed to get through the conversations' challenging points. Having a purpose that individuals care about helps them feel they have some skin in the game and intrinsic motivation to do whatever it takes to get the work done.

**Plan: Winging It Won't Win It**

Having a plan, or agenda, for your discussion is simply table stakes for running a good meeting. It's most common to think about the work product and deliverables. While this is necessary, we often don't consider the quality of the relationships and communication that will get the work done well, with the level of creativity and innovative thinking it might require. What distinguishes Conversations that Count is not just what people do as a result of the meeting, but how do they feel? How motivated and inspired are they to contribute their best? How well do they feel supported and that others have their back? Are they willing to go above and beyond and look out for one another?

***Step Into Their Shoes***

Stephen Covey's principle of "Begin with the end in mind" provides a good framework for a Conversation Leader. This principle is based on imagination – "the ability to envision in your mind what you cannot at present see with your eyes. It is based on the principle that all things are created twice. There is a mental (first) creation, and a physical (second) creation. The physical creation follows the mental, just as a building follows a blueprint." (Covey, n.d.)

By clarifying how you want the meeting to end, you can reverse-engineer the design and support needed to arrive at that desired destination.

In the Calibrate step of the COUNT model, you created an intention for how you, as leader of the conversation, want to show up. In the Orient step, it's time to step into your attendees' shoes and imagine what perspectives and issues they may bring to the table. Shift your perspective from preparing yourself, to seeing the meeting through the lens of your participants and their needs and desires.

Set an intention for the experience of your participants. Authors Chad Littlefield and Will Wise say, "Intention is connected to purpose, and yet it is so much more than that. The root *intendere*, from Latin, suggests "to stretch," so when you make an intention, you are inviting yourself (and others) to stretch, grow and evolve toward something greater, to something purposeful." (Wise & Littlefield, 2017).

At the end of the meeting, how do you want them to feel about their contribution? How do you hope they will regard their role in the team? What shift do you wish to see in their willingness to do what it takes to get the work done?

Make how you work together as important as the work itself. Taking time to reflect on the experience you desire for your participants helps tap into empathy, supports your listening, and puts you in a place of deeper connection to the people you serve by leading a Conversation that Counts.

**Create an Ecosystem for Connection**

Working remotely for such a prolonged period even has some introverts wistful for the days when you could sit down with your colleagues in a room for a chat. Just as you want participants to connect to the purpose and context of your work, you'll want them to relate to each other as well. Create a personal connection time, whether it's five minutes for a few personal shares or asking people to share in the online chat. Asking how they are doing or their intention for the discussion helps participants shift from whatever they were doing before the meeting and become fully present.

When people meet in person, there is a natural transition time to shift their focus to the meeting. People settle into their chairs, have that first sip of coffee, and have a quick chat with the people sitting next to them. Conversation Leaders use that unstructured time to welcome people, review the agenda, and launch into the first discussion item. The individual participant's energy is sustained and fed by being in the physical presence of their colleagues. In a survey of meeting science, researcher and author Joseph Allen found that small-talk actually supports better business outcomes and successful meetings than more structured work talk or preparatory remarks about a meeting. "Shooting the breeze with your colleagues, even just for a minute or two before diving into work talk, can make for a better meeting," Allen advises (Reed & Allen, 2021).

From participating in and witnessing hundreds of virtual meetings over the pandemic, I've noticed an important shift in managing participant energy that is different from an in-person meeting. In virtual meetings, that unstructured small-talk connection time typically doesn't happen. People log in, the meeting leaders wait in silence until the clock indicates it's time to start, and then the meeting begins. It may sound efficient, but it's not very welcoming. In a virtual meeting space, you can't have that spontaneous chat at the coffee station or as you take your seat. Without those warm-up conversations, participants can feel isolated. Connecting strengthens relationships and adds much-needed energy to the meeting.

### *Have a Dynamic Game Plan*

When it comes to the substantive issues of your discussion, you need a clearly defined game plan that is also adaptable, so you can shift and meet the needs of the moment. Focus the discussion with an agenda – this gives people a roadmap of what they can expect to cover and helps them manage their attention and energy accordingly. Perhaps you start with an agenda created and shared in advance, then modify it with your participants' input. It is a starting point and should serve as a guide for organizing your time in the meeting.

Don't expect your agenda to unfold exactly as planned, however. When it comes to group dynamics, you can expect a few curveballs, detours, and unexpected bumps on the road. For an emerging Conversation Leader struggling to get the group on-topic it might be more important to throw out your pre-designed agenda and just listen to what needs are emerging within your group. This part of the meeting can feel messy and confronting. It is completely normal that the conversation isn't always linear, differences of opinions get expressed, and people aren't sure what to do next. "Building shared understanding is a struggle, not a platitude," says author and facilitator Sam Kaner. "Misunderstanding and miscommunication are normal, natural aspects of participatory decision-making." (Kaner, 2014).

Creating an agenda in chunks that can be delivered and discussed in shorter periods can be particularly useful for virtual meetings. Modularizing your discussion topics provides the flexibility to shift and adapt based on what the group needs. Like LEGO bricks, some basic forms of content or ideas can be put together in many ways and sequences, depending on what you're trying to build. When leading a discussion virtually, you need the ability to adapt quickly to respond to the group's attention span and engagement, and stay focused on the tasks at hand.

Running a great meeting is like baking a cake; it takes heat and time. Repeatedly opening the oven to see if it's done yet reduces the temperature and increases your baking time. Conversations will sometimes feel heated, or messy, or unformed. But if you're clear on your purpose, foster strength in relationships, and allow the group's wisdom to play out, you will have an effective and engaging conversation.

### Parts: Have Everything in Its Place

Another important aspect is to create an environment that is supportive and conducive to discussion. As we saw in the Ballroom story that opened this chapter, it's essential to have a meeting space that supports safety and intimacy, so participants feel free to speak up and engage fully in honest and vulnerable conversations.

As the Conversation Leader, your role is to set the table for the feast of ideas, discussion, understanding and connection. In cooking, chefs follow the principle of "mise en place", which means putting everything in place before you begin making the dish. You read the recipe and prepare your workspace. Carrots and onions are chopped and measured into individual bowls, spices are measured, pans prepared, and the oven pre-heated. Although it takes practice, "mise en place" makes meal preparation simple. You have exactly what you need when you need it.

You are like a chef when you lead a Conversation that Counts. There are ingredients you'll want consistently, and there may be new things to introduce or source depending on the nature of your conversation. Your meeting environment – whether in-person or virtual – sets a tone that has an important impact on how well you're able to connect and converse together.

It's up to you to ensure you have everything that supports the conversational space you wish to create. Some essential parts of every meeting include:

#### *Welcoming Work Environment*

Where will the meeting take place? Pay attention to the ambience you create. A meeting in a sun-filled room with comfortable seating and décor will have a different impact than meeting in the basement or a windowless hotel room, with an accordion divider on one side and stackable, uncomfortable chairs. For in-person sessions, having a well-lit room, spacious enough for people to move around, ideally with a view of or easy access to the outdoors, is best.

Consider different ways to do your work together. Can people work in pairs, triads, or small groups at some points? How can you get people to shift their physical position (sitting, standing, moving about the room)? Design your meeting environment to serve the purpose of the group.

In virtual meetings, the same principles apply. You'll want to ensure you use a video conferencing platform that is reliable and easy to use for your participants. In this case, you may need to plan for pre-session orientation videos or handouts on how to navigate the technology.

Depending on the kind of virtual conversation you're leading, consider webinar or discussion mode options. A webinar is typically better suited for presentations to groups of people, as it keeps the focus on the main presenters and channels contributions from audience members into questions for the speaker. People cannot see or communicate with others in attendance, thus maintaining focus on the presentation and minimizing distractions. Meeting mode offers the group choices that better mimic a traditional in-person meeting, with breakout spaces, participant chats, and the ability to use some collaborative and interactive tools such as whiteboards, polling, and annotation.

With your chosen videoconferencing tools, consider how to put people into breakout rooms of any size to allow for small group sharing. Use the chatbox to support the connection between participants and as a way to contribute your voice, rather than just speaking at people and taking turns speaking one at a time. There are multiple communication channels available when working virtually – from sharing emoji reactions, sending group or private chat, raising your hand, asking questions and more.

**Clear Expectations**

An essential part of creating your conversational space is deciding, articulating, and aligning the expectations. If people come to a meeting expecting to contribute their ideas and instead find themselves on the receiving end of multiple PowerPoint presentations with little time for discussion, there is a mismatch between their expectation and their experience. Your participants will be confused about their role. Mismatches and unfulfilled expectations lead to cynicism and meeting fatigue.

> It's not just the destination that's important; it's how we get there. We take the journey together.

Engagement improves when expectations are shared. It may not be necessary for a weekly stand-up meeting, but can be incredibly useful when you need to launch a new project or re-think the work you're doing as the result of a new priority or problem. Take the time upfront to talk about participants' roles, why it matters that they are there, and the importance and value of their contribution.

Start your meeting with clarity about its objective and your plan to tackle the agenda. In my training as a Team Performance Practitioner with The Grove Consultants International, I found their OARRS framework to be very helpful (Sibbett, 2021).

## O – Objectives

This is a statement of the key desired outcomes for the meeting. In helping clients design impactful sessions, I have found that if that the objective can't be stated clearly or succinctly, there could be too much going on for a single meeting.

## A – Agenda

This is the planned schedule for when you'll discuss items, and for how long. Even an initial understanding of the timeframe for a particular part of the agenda conveys its priority. This helps participants to marshal their time, energy and attention accordingly. Sharing the agenda in advance enables participants to prepare.

Be sure to include planned breaks in the agenda. At in-person meetings, it's easy to stand up, grab that second cup of coffee, and get a stretch break at the same time. Virtual meetings are often densely planned with minimal breaks. You may want to incorporate a quick collective stretch break before moving from one topic to the next. Our brains need a break from the screen, and giving people permission to stand up and move about helps change their state and re-energize them for the next portion of the discussion.

## R – Roles

Here we confirm who is in the room and what their expected role will be. For a regular team discussion, you can rotate the roles of timekeeper or note taker among the team. In a virtual meeting, you may have additional people in your space to help you run the session, like a Zoom host, virtual facilitator, or a special guest. Be sure that everyone knows who is in the room.

When leading Conversations that Count, I also find it useful to speak to your role as the Conversation Leader. Sometimes you'll want to speak up and offer your perspective, but be aware of the authority that is naturally invested in you because you're leading the discussion. Your words (and even reactions to other people's input) carry much weight and have a disproportionate impact on how others participate.

It is also helpful to let people know you will wear different hats during the discussion. One of your hats is that of the Conversation Leader, who needs to orchestrate the discussion, ensure all views are heard and help ensure the group meets the outcomes on time. Another hat you may wear is that of a team member, where you speak from your experience, informed by your position before being promoted to the manager role. Distinguishing which hat you are wearing when you talk helps people feel that "input" offered while wearing your participant hat doesn't get confused with "direction" given under the Conversation Leader hat.

**R – Rules**

Determine what kinds of agreements, codes of conduct or rules of behaviour will support a successful meeting. Examples could include being on time for meetings or listening first without interrupting others. You may request that people who are critical of something prepare constructive alternatives. You may have rules from previous discussions that worked well that you'll want to continue. These rules provide a set of agreements that define and set mutual expectations of how you work together. Remember, they can be refined and adjusted as needed.

*Timing*

Meetings often are maligned because it's rare to be in one where you leave feeling more energized and productive than when you walked in. According to Reed and Allen, there is ample academic literature on meeting science that bears out what our experience tells us to be true: "there is widespread inefficiency in workplace meetings" (Reed & Allen, 2021). Organizations in the United States waste over $200 billion a year on "ineffective, suboptimal and/or poor meetings" (Keith, 2015).

Start your meetings by appreciating everyone for showing up. A little bit of gratitude and acknowledgement for the priorities people had to juggle to attend goes a long way. Respect people's time by beginning on time. Don't erode goodwill and attention by waiting for that one last person who is perpetually late for everything to arrive. As the Conversation Leader, be ready early so you can set up for the meeting and connect with people – whether you're meeting in person or virtually.

Assess what you can get done in the time available as you approach the promised end time. Don't assume "just another 20 minutes or so" will be acceptable to everyone. Particularly with people working at home, juggling children and other family responsibilities, their schedules are finely tuned. If that cartoon show was strategically chosen to keep a little one occupied until Daddy got off his meeting, then deciding to extend the meeting an extra few minutes without everyone's agreement can throw other obligations out of balance.

"The first step in improving meetings is to make them places of refuge and opportunity rather than wells of lost time and energy," conclude Reed and Allen (Reed & Allen, 2021). Even though people may report to you, be respectful of their time. As the Conversation Leader, you set the bar for how people show up and treat one another.

## Tips for Virtual Conversations

In the Orient phase, you've shifted your perspective from what it will take to prepare you to lead the meeting to what is needed to create a welcoming and safe environment for your participants to have an experience where they leave feeling aligned, clear on next steps, and understanding how to contribute their skills to the team. Here are a few issues that deserve your attention and care when leading a virtual conversation.

### 💡 *Bring in the Participant's Voice*

It's important to be sure you bring the participants into your conversations, particularly if you are meeting virtually. Give careful consideration to how you create space in the discussion for your participants to contribute. Is a 45-minute presentation delivered with PowerPoint, followed by a 10-minute question and answer period, really the best and only way to engage people and get their input? Likely not. More importantly, it postpones bringing the participant's voice into the conversation until later, which distances their experience and connection to the meeting. Conversations that Count are impactful and indispensable because the participant's voice is valued, sought after, and integral to the conversation.

Be sure to create a space to hear from people right at the beginning. Don't wait until you're halfway through the meeting to invite people to use the chat, or schedule a breakout session to mix it up a bit. Give people a chance at the beginning to gather to welcome each other and share how they're feeling. Have those moments be that casual coffee chat conversation that we don't get any more when we're not in rooms together.

Make sure you build in time early in your meeting to hear from people just on a casual basis. Then you can transition into the formal part of your actual agenda.

### 💡 Reduce Friction of Connection

Establish a meeting norm that cameras stay on during your discussion. Naturally, there might be those exceptional circumstances when a camera may need to be switched off momentarily while your teenager comes out of the shower forgetting you're on a call and wanders through your background. But encourage people to stay visible during your meetings. According to authors Reed and Allen, "If someone can see you speaking, you have humanized the message and made it much more likely to be remembered." (Reed & Allen, 2021). It helps foster a sense of connection, supported accountability for staying active in the meeting, and also gives you a window into people's body language and demeanour that helps you read the room.

A standard protocol for large gatherings is to have people stay on mute unless they want to share. That works well because seeing someone come off mute is an indicator that they are ready to speak, so you can spot them quickly and call on them directly. However, having to turn on and off your mute button does create a bit of friction. For meetings with ten or fewer participants, I like to encourage that people keep the audio live. This practice better mimics the dynamics of an in-person meeting where you can hear the murmurs of agreements or laughter at your jokes. It can help inject some energy and banter into the virtual meeting room. Consider how you create space in the discussion for your participants to contribute.

Of course, if Fido starts to bark at the delivery of your next Amazon package, you can temporarily mute yourself.

## 💡 Prime the Pump

To make the most of your time together, prepare your participants for success before the meeting even starts. Prime the pump for effective participation by ensuring everyone has the agenda, and share your expectations for the kind of participation you'll need from them. Think about what you can do before the meeting starts to prepare them to be engaged, focussed, energized and connected to each subject. It could be to send out a pre-read, or a video to watch or share a few questions you want people to think about before they arrive. These kinds of actions help people get a head start on some of the pre-thinking and preparations for making the most use of your virtual meeting time.

One way to pare down virtual meeting agendas from the traditional in-person meetings is to think through what participants need to do together and what can be done independently on their own schedule. Synchronous activities, such as discussion and decision-making, are likely best done live together, particularly if you want to create a collaborative and participatory decision-making process. Asynchronous activities, such as pre-work reading or reflection, can be stripped out of the live meeting agenda and left to be done on their own time ahead of the meeting itself. While you'll likely have to review pre-work material since inevitably some won't have done it, you can still streamline your virtual meeting agenda by keeping the main thing as the main thing in your live interactions.

## 💡 Relationships Trump Technology

It's unclear how long we'll be in mostly virtual meetings and conversations, so we have to adapt fully to this virtual way of working together. More meetings will become hybrid in future, where some of the team meets in person and others will be on video conference. We are fortunate to have so many tools to choose from.

Relationships trump technology. Great technology will never replace or be more important than the quality of our relationships. We need to keep the mission and the purpose of our work close to our core; otherwise, we risk virtual meetings becoming transactional, rather than opportunities to create something that can transform our clients' lives, the kind of work we do in the world and the meaning that we get from it.

Just because there is a fancy new virtual platform doesn't mean you should use it. "Finding the right meeting space is now using the right meeting software," say authors Reed and Allen (Reed & Allen, 2021). Be intentional about whether it serves to strengthen the quality of relationships and add value to your conversation or whether the learning curve is simply a distraction.

To ensure that unfamiliarity with technology doesn't become a barrier to engagement, think through what's needed for your participants to fully participate. Consider how you can help them be successful in connecting to the virtual meeting technology, and don't make assumptions that everyone is skilled or proficient. Nothing deflates group energy faster at the start of a meeting than a few people struggling to find their mute button, turn their cameras on, or are unable to find the "raise hand" button so they can ask a question.

Prepare an onboarding video or FAQ sheet to help your team understand how best to use the virtual technologies. Using a new online collaboration tool? Create a practice space and short introductory video so people can give it a whirl and ensure they can connect properly in advance of the meeting.

## Take Action

> ### ORIENT INGREDIENTS
>
> **More of:**
> - ☑ Define purpose — keep your eyes on the prize
> - ☑ Set an intention for the group — step into their shoes
> - ☑ Plan a narrative
> - ☑ Design the environment
> - ☑ Reverse engineer to meet your outcome
>
> **Less of:**
> - ☒ Unclear expectations
> - ☒ Lack of connection points
> - ☒ Lack of clear roles
> - ☒ Run from discomfort
>
> **Add Your Own Ingredients:**
> _____
> _____
> _____
>
> **Watch Out For:**
> _____
> _____
> _____

### ✅ Meeting Gems

Think of meetings you've attended that had the greatest impact on you. Perhaps they inspired, or you learned something useful. How was that conversation run, and how was the meeting structured? What were three actions, choices or decisions that the Conversation Leader and the group did really well?

Three things that worked well

1. _____

2. _____

3. _____

## ✓ Meeting Pet Peeves

Now think about meetings you've experienced that were confusing or felt like a waste of your time. This is less about the subject matter and more about how the conversation was run. What are your three biggest pet peeves about meetings?

Three pet peeves

1. _____

2. _____

3. _____

## ✓ Rules of Engagement

What ground rules would you like to have in the conversations you run? What expectations do you want to set for how your team works together?

_____
_____
_____
_____
_____

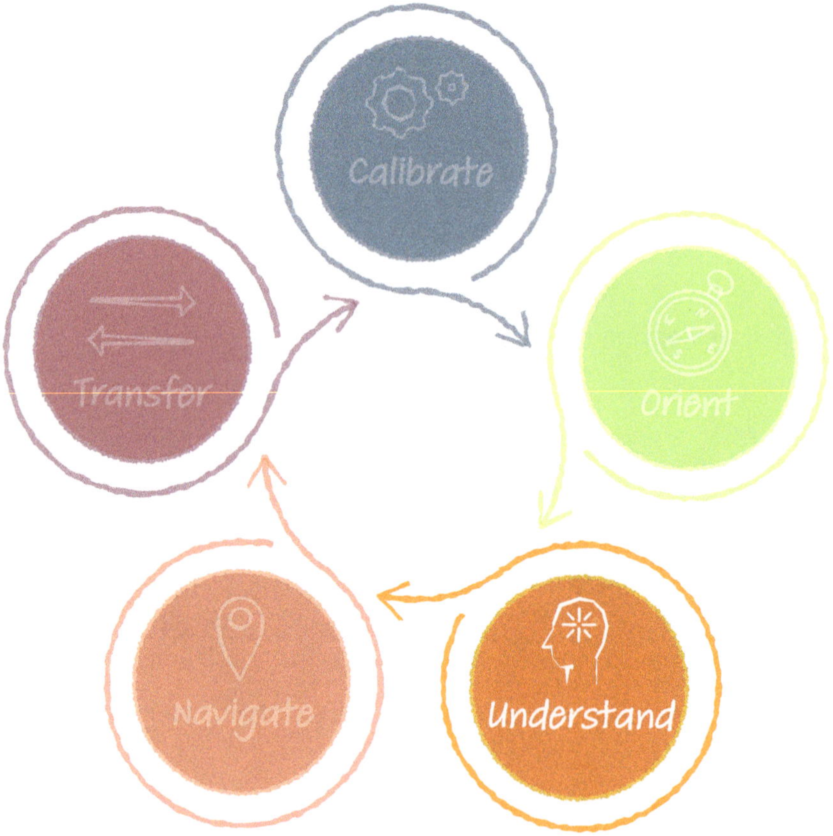
Calibrate
Orient
Understand
Navigate
Transfer

# CHAPTER FIVE

# Understand

*We are each other's harvest; we are each other's business; we are each other's magnitude and bond.*

– *Gwendolyn Brooks*

**Are You Finding Solutions for the Wrong Problem?**

Several years ago, I decided to take up running. While I had been athletic growing up, my favourite activities were team sports, particularly volleyball. As I got older, started my own business, and raised my three children, it became too challenging to find eleven people willing to play some pick-up volleyball with me.

I looked for an activity that would give me the cardiovascular workout I needed, so I joined a local running store to start my running career on the right footing (see what I did there?). The store had a great program where they offered group courses and taught you how to run, slowly building up your endurance and strength while managing the mental gremlins that constantly told me I didn't really like this running thing.

I gamely began the running program and was soon running a minimum of three times a week. I even entered a few five-kilometre races and started to think about upping my running career and training for a half marathon. But after about a year of running, I began to get sharp pains in my right foot, particularly when I woke up in the morning. According to the consensus of my running friends and Dr Google, I had likely developed plantar fasciitis.

The pain rapidly curtailed my running, and at times even walking was painful. Finding a solution became imperative. Initially, I started with an orthotic recommended by my chiropractor. After a few weeks, I didn't notice any change in my pain, and there was still no way I could run. Massage therapy alleviated the pain temporarily, but it always came back. I went to my family doctor, who diagnosed plantar fasciitis, and recommended a chiropodist. The foot specialist also diagnosed plantar fasciitis and charged me almost $1,000 for custom orthotics made from a mold of my feet. A few months after trying custom-made orthotics, I was still having pain.

After almost two years of nearly chronic pain in my right leg and mounting frustration, a friend recommended I go and see her applied kinesiologist. Desperate, I booked an appointment without really knowing what an applied kinesiologist did. I mentioned the upcoming appointment to my sister, who is a veterinarian and epidemiologist by training, and she said, "Isn't that the same foot you broke eight years ago?" I had totally forgotten that I had broken my fifth metatarsal bone years earlier. After six weeks in a walking cast, the bone had apparently healed up nicely, so I thought nothing further of it.

When I went to the kinesiologist, he used muscle testing as a way to assess my leg. I mentioned to him about that foot having been broken several years earlier. "I don't know if there is any connection to what's going on now though," I confessed. He looked at me intently, his eyebrows raised, and he tested my leg muscles. Within 30 seconds, he had an answer. "Your current pain has everything to do with you having broken your foot. Your tendons on the outside are stretched, and your arch has been compressed. As a result, your tibia and fibula aren't hitting your heel plate properly. Everything in your leg has been compensating for that injury since then."

I had a flash of anger at the doctors who oversaw my broken foot. When deemed "healed" I'd asked if any physiotherapy or reconditioning was needed and was assured, "Just walk on it, you'll be fine." Yet here I was, years later and in chronic pain from that injury. "But these orthotics were created for me by a foot specialist," I insisted. The kinesiologist muscle tested me wearing the orthotics. "You can throw them away," he said. "They are a solution to a problem you don't have."

Instead, he taped my foot and leg to support my body to re-learn proper alignment when walking. I was highly skeptical because the tape didn't seem to be doing much. Yet two days later, I was walking pain-free for the first time in two years.

## We Live in a VUCA World

We live in a complex and rapidly changing world, where we constantly encounter issues that challenge our expertise and experience. Solving the mystery of my foot pain showed that it took two years to identify and address the root cause of the problem despite tapping into specialist expertise. It's one thing to come up with a solution and take action, but what if you're not addressing the core problem to begin with? There are immense costs and consequences when we make an effort to find and implement a solution, only to find it's ineffective, obsolete or creates unforeseen consequences that spiral out a whole new set of issues.

There has perhaps never been a greater need for people to come together to solve truly dire and complex problems. It has almost become a cliché, but we do live in a VUCA world – volatile, uncertain, complex and ambiguous. The term came into use in 1987 to describe general conditions and situations, but the U.S. Army War College used it as a framework to describe a shift in geopolitical structure resulting from the end of the Cold War.

VUCA migrated to organizational boardrooms as companies and governments alike grappled with issues of strategic leadership in the 21$^{st}$ century. Consider the scope of change we've experienced globally, even in the year 2020 alone, to get a sense of the events and shifts that VUCA well describes:

- Devastating wildfires in Australia and the western coast of the United States, and an enormous glacier breaking up in the Antarctic, providing further evidence of the impact of unchecked global climate change.
- The rapid spread of COVID-19 around the globe, with its resulting and continuing massive shifts in how we work, live and socialize.
- The rise of social movements, such as Black Live Matters or #MeToo, that shed light on persistent systemic structures of racism, sexism and exclusion in modern society.
- Shifting geopolitical alliances, such as the Brexit vote and years of protracted negotiation and uncertainty as the United Kingdom left the European Union.
- A widening gap in income where, according to the World Economic Forum, the world's 2,153 billionaires have more than the 4.6 billion people who make up 60 percent of the planet's population (Oxfam International, 2020). The pandemic notwithstanding, Forbes reports that the world's billionaires were worth $11.4 trillion in 2020, up 20 percent from 2019 (Peterson-Withorn, 2020).

This list alone shows the complexity and scope of some of the more global issues we face. These issues have an array of intersectional, complicated, and systemic structures that defy simple and superficial answers. Understanding the root causes needs our best thinking if we're to have any hope of tackling these imbalances and threats.

## The Essentials Skills of Understand

The Understand component of the Conversations that Count framework comes down to three essential skills that are a minimum requirement for an impactful discussion: Listen, Learn and Leverage.

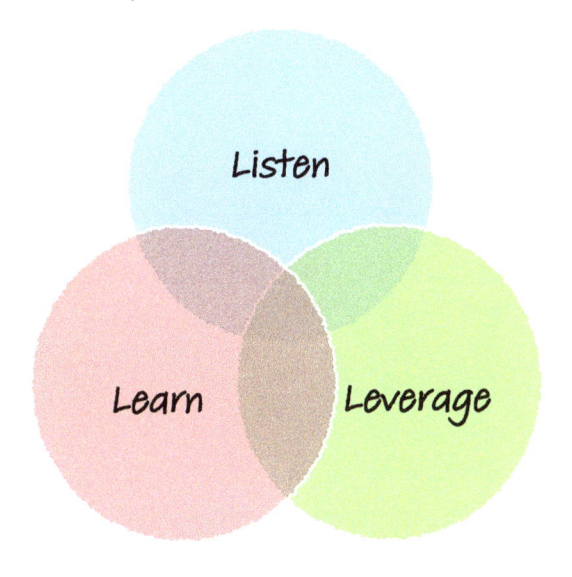

*Figure 6: Understand Strategies*

### Listen: Be Aware of How You Listen

***Listening is Key to Leading Effective Conversations***

When we hear the word conversation, we think of witty repartee, dialogue and how we express ourselves verbally. But the magic of impactful conversations has far more to do with how well we listen to one another. Think of the last time you had a discussion where you walked away feeling deeply understood, inspired or reassured. Chances are you experienced a quality of listening where you felt truly seen, heard, and respected for who you are.

Listening feels like it should be a natural skill, but it isn't. Too often – particularly in the workplace – we think that we're listening when we're only listening to judge, compare other's thoughts to our own, or simply prepare to continue expressing our views. It's natural to listen through our filters, biases, experiences and agendas.

As the Conversation Leader, the ability to listen is key to leading effective conversations. When you leave space for others to speak, you'll find they'll be more inclined to contribute and engage.

> Listening to respond is not the same as listening to understand.

How are you building in time to listen and get feedback and input? Recently, I was on a call with about 150 people. They had a breakout session so people could speak in smaller groups, which was great. I love using breakout sessions because they're a great way to help people make that personal relationship and communicate with each other.

But when it came back to the plenary, the meeting leader asked simply, "Who has something they'd like to say?" That meant only one or two people, out of 150, were able to share. There was no further instruction about how people would be called upon and no invitation made for how else others could share. Plus, there were only ten minutes left at this point in the meeting, so it was clear the "sharing" in the large group wasn't being given a high priority. With the lack of instruction and the short time frame, the large group was relatively silent and passive. Without some designed structure for sharing, people's views were pretty much sidelined.

Imagine what might have been possible if that leader had instead said, "I want to hear from one or two of you in the time we have left, but I want to invite all of you to give us one key insight you got from your breakout. Put it in the chat so that we can read through that. We'll also make the chat available to you all after the call, so you can learn from each other and bring back some of the insights to your team members who weren't at this session. But I'm going to call on a couple of you directly so that we can speak. Let me know you'd like to share by clicking the "raise hand" button at the bottom of your screen." By acknowledging the time and structure constraints and providing clear instructions for participating in the sharing, everyone in the session is acknowledged and included. It's a way to leverage engagement and becomes a conversation with everybody, rather than watching a show of two or three people talking to each other. When people feel like they are participating actively, you will get a much better return on your investment of people's time, energy, attention, goodwill and productivity.

Being able to listen deeply requires you to recognize the filters that may influence your ability to understand another point of view and intentionally set them aside, at least temporarily. In the Calibrate stage, the Conversation Leader adopts a mindset of curiosity to set aside potential biases and blind spots that may adversely impact their ability to stay present and listen to what's being said.

When you're confident in leading the conversation, you know it's less about what you need to say and more about how much you need to listen. Listening builds trust, connection and commitment.

### Listen with Your Gut

Listening is not just something you do with your ears. Trust your gut, not just your meeting agenda. Feelings are every bit as important as facts. Listening to your gut helps you detect and address shifting group dynamics.

Listen beyond the words to the energy used to deliver them. Use your eyes to pick up shifts in people's body language and facial expressions. Nonverbal communication is a big part of how we operate. Body language, gestures, facial expression, tone, pace, and voice modulation provide useful information.

Limiting to a square box view of someone's shoulders and head means many of the traditional cues of body language unconsciously used to ascertain meaning are lost. You can't tell if someone has crossed their arms and is pushing back from the table. It's hard to detect if someone is multi-tasking and checking their email inbox instead of paying attention. You may miss the rolling eyes or raised eyebrows as your brain constantly scans the sea of little boxes of your colleagues onscreen. Tuning in to all your senses – auditory, visual, sensory – is even more crucial now that so many organizations must do their work on virtual platforms. Use all your senses to help pick up some of the more subtle communication signals from your participants.

### Learn: Understanding Takes Effort

Context provides a framework and perspective for how we listen, work, and think together. Conversation is better with a shared sense of the context in which it takes place.

I remember watching the movie *Saturday Night Fever* (Saturday Night Fever, 1977) when it was first released. The film is about Tony Manero, a young man growing up in Brooklyn, struggling between the joyous highs and accolades he receives on the disco dance floor and the lows of his dispiriting, day-to-day reality living at home with a dead-end job and few prospects for his future. I found it a very poignant film, and I felt much empathy for Tony and his friends. (And I enjoyed the disco music and dancing too!)

Some 20 years later, I watched the movie again with a friend who'd never seen it. While my reaction was similar to the first time, my friend thought it was a decent comedy and that the filmmaker had made a pretty good spoof of life in New York in the 1970s. I explained that it was supposed to be a drama, not a comedy. "I didn't get that at all!" insisted my friend.

We watched the same movie, but with a totally different understanding of its intention. My friend assumed it was a recent movie, which led him to feel it was a sly comedy or "mockumentary". Once he understood the context – that the film was made in 1977 and depicted current events of that era – my friend started to see how the film could be construed as a drama.

Context provides the framework and foundation for your work together and why it even matters. Ensuring employees understand the company's mission and values are an important context for the work they do. Without context, they are left to make their own interpretations and assumptions, just like my friend watching the movie without an understanding of its origin.

"Leaders have to place strategic changes, initiatives, and goals into a broader organizational context, or they risk losing good talent, burning out managers, and wasting money on programs that don't pay off," argues author Ron Ashkenas. "People have to see why what they're doing has to change." (Ashkenas, 2015). Sharing changes in strategic directions or educating everyone on the nature of market challenges or disruptions to business as usual helps your team understand the importance and urgency of the meetings themselves.

### Silence Speaks Volumes

One mistake I've seen many Conversation Leaders make is in dealing with silence. They ask a question, and all they hear are crickets. Papers shuffle, people look away or stare intently someplace other than the Conversation Leader. Yet silence is often very beneficial to a group conversation. In our fast-paced, results-focused world, silence can feel confronting and even unproductive. However, silence gives participants a chance to reflect, digest what's been said, and create space for new connections or insights to emerge.

Conversation is like a glass of red wine. When you create time and space, meetings can be much more enjoyable! Red wine tastes better with aeration that allows the tannins to soften and the flavours to mellow. Sure, you can glug a glass of undecanted red wine with no problem. But appreciating its full flavor requires time.

It's hard to make conversations count when you're deluging people with content and not building in time, space, or opportunity for dialogue. I regard silence as an opportunity for the group to breathe in their inquiries. Rushing to a solution or action without taking time to marinate in the complexity and discomfort of problems can mean you miss important nuances and clues for tackling an issue.

Silence can also signal that the direction of the discussion is simply not resonating for some reason. Rather than force a conversation, just name the dynamic that you, as Conversation Leader, see happening. "I noticed we all got very silent. I'm curious about that. Who would like to share?" is a simple way to offer the group to observe its own dynamic and reaction, and help them go deeper to the heart of the matter.

## The Sound of Silence is Different in Virtual Meetings

An important difference between in-person and virtual meetings is the way people interpret silence. When you encounter silence in person, you can more readily detect if someone is in thought or not connecting to what you're talking about. A pause in conversation may even feel meaningful and significant, potentially even marking an important turning point in the conversation.

Silence is perceived differently in a virtual environment and more readily makes people feel anxious. The first thought is, "Uh oh, did I lose my audio?" rather than "Wow, that is so important to understand." According to Gianpiero Petriglieri, an associate professor at Insead, "Silence creates a natural rhythm in a real-life conversation. However, when it happens in a video call, you become anxious about the technology." (Jiang, 2020).

To compound this, a 2014 German study found that delays on phone or conferencing systems negatively shaped our views of people – "even delays of 1.2 seconds made people perceive the responder as less friendly or focused." (Katrin Schoenenberg, 2014).

To harness the power of silence in a virtual conversation, you need to frame it more explicitly than in person. You could set participants up to expect silence by saying, "Let's take a moment to let that sink in, and reflect what that means. You can use the chatbox to share what you think about this issue first, and then we'll discuss it together." You can normalize and acknowledge silence by saying, "I'm noticing a bit of a pause

> right now. I'm curious what you think about that. Who would like to share first?"

**Reflect and Iterate**

To deepen understanding, include time for self-reflection. In a group discussion, assess what's working, what's not, and what needs to be improved or different going forward. This way, your team can continuously improve and learn together.

However, you must also commit to your self-reflection and learning – it's easier once you've adopted a mindset of curiosity and humility. After all, who knows what you will discover, and you might even learn something you're not happy about. But the potential of not liking the results is not an excuse for skipping out on an opportunity to learn, and it is incongruous to set an expectation that your team should learn and improve, and not do so yourself. Research shows reflecting on lessons learned at the end of the day enhances performance and even happiness (Porter, 2017).

> # Follow effective action with quiet reflection, from the quiet reflection will come even more effective action.
>
> *– Peter Drucker*

**Leverage: There's Wisdom in the Room**

When you lead Conversations that Count, you leverage the collective wisdom, experience and perspectives of everyone in the room. No one has all the answers; we only hold one piece of the puzzle. When everyone puts their pieces on the table, we start to see and understand the picture together.

> None of us is as smart as all of us.
>
> *– Ken Blanchard*

***Acknowledge Others***

Acknowledging people's contributions and perspectives confirms that they were heard and valued. It's how we demonstrate respect. Have you ever spoken up to give an idea, and the Conversation Leader just continued? Whether your idea was ignored entirely, or the group leader ran with it without even a nod in your direction, the lack of acknowledgement creates disconnection and a disinclination to offer your input as freely or enthusiastically the next time. A simple "Thank you for that contribution!" or referring back to you as the originator of the initiative as the conversation evolves will often suffice. Don't take others for granted. Regularly acknowledging their input helps ensure you'll continue to get it.

Be mindful of how you acknowledge others, particularly when you are leading the conversation. You have significant positional authority, and your response can easily skew the way people interact. For example, I was working with a client I'll call Lara, who was facilitating a senior leadership team meeting to tackle challenging staffing and funding issues. Lara had structured the agenda and asked who had ideas to offer. Joe spoke up and suggested one solution. "That's a great idea!" exclaimed Lara. She then started to ask Joe for more details on how his solution might work, as Joe's colleagues around the table nodded their heads. After Lara and Joe finished their discussion, Lara turned to the rest of the group and asked, "Who else has an idea?" Tamar raised her hand and gave a different idea. "Ok, I guess that might work," Lara said. She tapped her pen against her paper and then asked, "Who else has something to offer?" I wasn't the only person to see Tamar's shoulders slump as she pushed her chair back slightly from the meeting table.

Lara's role was to support a conversation among the members of the senior leadership team. Yet the way she acknowledged each idea clearly telegraphed how she judged its merits. Instead of a group discussion, Lara turned the conversation into a series of one-to-one chats with a specific person on the team while everyone else watched. Instead of managing the conversation space, Lara had put herself in the centre, acting as the traffic cop on people's ideas, deciding which had merit and which didn't.

Judging and evaluating input leads to performative participation, not innovation or breakthrough thinking. Anything you say in response to a contribution, whether positive or negative, will impact the group as a whole, not just the individual who contributed.

### Convergent and Divergent Thinking: Don't Cross the Streams

There's a time for blue-sky thinking, brainstorming and idea generation. And there's a time for making choices, setting priorities, and separating what's mission-critical from ideas for another time. Knowing when to shift from one thought process to another can feel messy, confusing and confronting. This is where your surfing skills will be tested.

The transition between convergent and divergent thinking is known by facilitators as "The Groan Zone". As Kaner says, "building shared understanding is a struggle, not a platitude". It's the messy middle where some people want to keep coming up with ideas, while others are ready to get down to brass tacks and make choices.

Learn to get comfortable with being uncomfortable. The Groan Zone is a natural dynamic of group discussion. "When people experience discomfort in the midst of a group decision-making process, they often take it as evidence that their group is dysfunctional. As their impatience increases so does their disillusionment with the process," says Kaner. "Misunderstanding and miscommunication are normal, natural aspects of participatory decision-making. The Groan Zone is a direct, inevitable consequence of the diversity that exists in any group. Working through these misunderstandings builds the foundation for sustainable agreements. Without shared understanding, meaningful collaboration is impossible." (Kaner, 2014).

In the iconic film *Ghostbusters*, there's a scene where the Ghostbusting team arrives onsite to de-ghostify a New York City hotel. Their new proton-pack guns are tested for the first time, and they emit a ray that will zap a ghost into a containment box. Before they burst into a haunted ballroom to bust up the apparitions that have terrorized the hotel guests, Egon Spengler (played by Harold Ramis) warns his team not to cross the streams when zapping apparitions. When asked why they shouldn't, his response is simply, "It would be...bad." (Ghostbusters, 1984).

That scene often pops into my mind when I'm in a facilitated session, and the person leading the discussion veers from generative, divergent conversation into convergent, "let's make some choices here" mode. A perspective met with an editorial comment such as, "Oh, well that's not really what we're focusing on now" or "That's a fantastic idea!" sends conflicting signals. Those comments signal a value judgment from the Conversation Leader. Your role is to spark, direct and create the environment for an engaged and enlightening discussion. Assessing ideas as they emerge tags some as better than others and works counter to the principle of tapping into the diversity of thought around the table.

Don't cross the streams. It would be bad.

**Ask Questions**

There is a lot of power and potential when we ask questions. As Hal Gregersen writes in his book, *Questions are the Answer*, "Questions have a curious power to unlock new insights and positive behavior change in every part of our lives. They can get people unstuck and open new directions for progress no matter what they are struggling with." (Gregerson, 2018).

> Without a good question, a good
> answer has no place to go.
>
> *– Michael Bungay Stanier*

Conversation Leaders would do well to step away from the temptation to have all the answers and, instead, ask more questions. Resist the allure of answering questions that arise naturally during discussion. Through the collective searching and wrestling to find answers, a group discovers what it's really capable of.

## Tips for Virtual Conversations

If you need input from the attendees, you'll need to think closely about how to design that into your virtual meeting. When we meet in person, sitting next to one another or across the table, the idea of sharing our ideas or asking questions was quite a natural process. Physical proximity, eye contact, and an ability to read body language and cues readily help us to do that.

In a virtual meeting, we need to articulate the norms and expectations more precisely and overtly. Even if you know everyone on the call, you need to overcome the sense of disconnection that may hold people back. Here are some guidelines to help you design for connection and engagement right from the start of your virtual meeting:

### 💡 Engage from the Start

How you start a meeting is critical because it sets an energetic tone and a space for the entire conversation. When we got together in person in physical rooms, the focus was not just about what we were talking about. It was also about the chance to meet other people, connect and network. Remember you'd get to the meeting a few minutes early, grab a coffee. You'd have a chat with somebody over a donut, and there'd be a little bit of catching up over what you did on the weekend. Then we would sit down and get the work done.

Now that we're in virtual rooms, we don't have the same opportunity for spontaneous human connection and conversations. We mustn't let our reliance on technology overshadow our need for that human touch, that human connection. There's nothing worse than coming into a meeting and you're met with a flat "Oh, hi!" and then silence until the meeting officially starts. That is very off-putting and deflating.

Have people listen to music when they're arriving, and welcome them as they get on. Use the chat function. Ask a question in the chat and have people chime in with answers to "Where are you calling from?", "How are you feeling today?" or "What's the best show you've seen lately?" Give them a simple activity. Maybe they need to reflect on the minutes or the materials that were sent out in advance of the meeting. Plan for something you can do to engage them right from the start, so they become what body language expert and author Mark Bowden calls "active participants rather than passive consumers" (Bowden, 2021). The energy and goodwill you generate in those early crucial moments goes a long way to build the momentum that will carry you through the entire discussion.

### 💡 Leverage multiple channels of communication

One of the wonderful advantages of videoconferencing platforms is that they allow for different channels of communication and participation. To the degree you can, what can you bring forward from your in-person meetings that worked well into your virtual meeting environment? The platforms that support remote work offer several ways to augment the best ways that we used to meet.

Regardless of an individual's preferred communication style, there is bound to be some way to encourage them to speak. For those who find it intimidating to speak up in a room full of extroverts with strong opinions, the chance to share ideas via chat or in smaller breakout spaces can work. Think beyond the typical setting of everyone being all onscreen at once and incorporate time to do some individual reflection or even paired sharing as a way to build connection, to share ideas, and to ensure that the participant voice is heard.

You can go beyond just verbal input as well. Use simple tools, such as the "reactions" button in Zoom or using stamps to annotate a slide to indicate a level of agreement with a certain position. Have people change their name to include a response to a question as a way to have everyone check in at the beginning and end of a meeting.

## 💡 Less is more

When it comes to planning, use the principle of "less is more". I've noticed in the past year of the pandemic that we've realized taking a one-day retreat and putting it into a one-day virtual format just doesn't work. People just can't. Their brains are mush by the time you hit the three-hour mark, or even sooner!

We understand that we have to make some time adjustments, but we need to take it even further. You can't cram a lot of content into a shorter period of time and expect to have the same quality of engagement and dialogue. It's like packing your suitcase for a long holiday and filling up two suitcases, and then deciding you don't want to check any bags. If you're taking fewer bags, you won't be able to take everything you had initially planned for, and need to pare back your clothing selections.

Focus on what is most essential in your team gathering. Maybe you can hive off some things and deal with them through email. Perhaps some are old protocol leftovers where people feel they have to show and tell to keep people up to date. There may be more effective ways of getting that across.

Once you've pared it down to the essentials, take a look at what you have. Then take it back even more – remove another 25 percent. That way you leave space for people to have a back and forth dialogue with each other, and time for less formal social chit chat and needed breaks. You leave some space for people to reflect and digest what they're hearing and be able to contribute.

## Take Action

> ### UNDERSTAND INGREDIENTS
>
> **More of:**
> - ☑ Listen to learn
> - ☑ Listen with your gut
> - ☑ Listen to silence
> - ☑ Share the context
> - ☑ Acknowledge others
> - ☑ Self reflection
> - ☑ Ask more questions
>
> **Less of:**
> - ☒ Listen to respond
> - ☒ Cram your agenda
> - ☒ Fill the silence with talking
> - ☒ Don't ask questions
> - ☒ Answer the questions that get asked
> - ☒ Cross the streams
>
> **Add Your Own Ingredients:**
> _____
> _____
> _____
>
> **Watch Out For:**
> _____
> _____
> _____

### ✓ Question Inventory

Create a list of ten powerful, open-ended questions that would help your group do its best work.

**Great questions I want to use.**

1. _____
2. _____
3. _____
4. _____
5. _____

6. _____

7. _____

8. _____

9. _____

10. _____

## ✓ Self-Reflection

After each conversation you lead, make time for some self-reflection – it doesn't have to be time-consuming or difficult. Even 15 minutes spent contemplating your answers to the following questions will be enormously helpful in developing your confidence to lead Conversations that Count.

**What worked well?**

_____

_____

_____

**What didn't work so well?**

_____

_____

_____

What would I do differently when leading my next conversation?

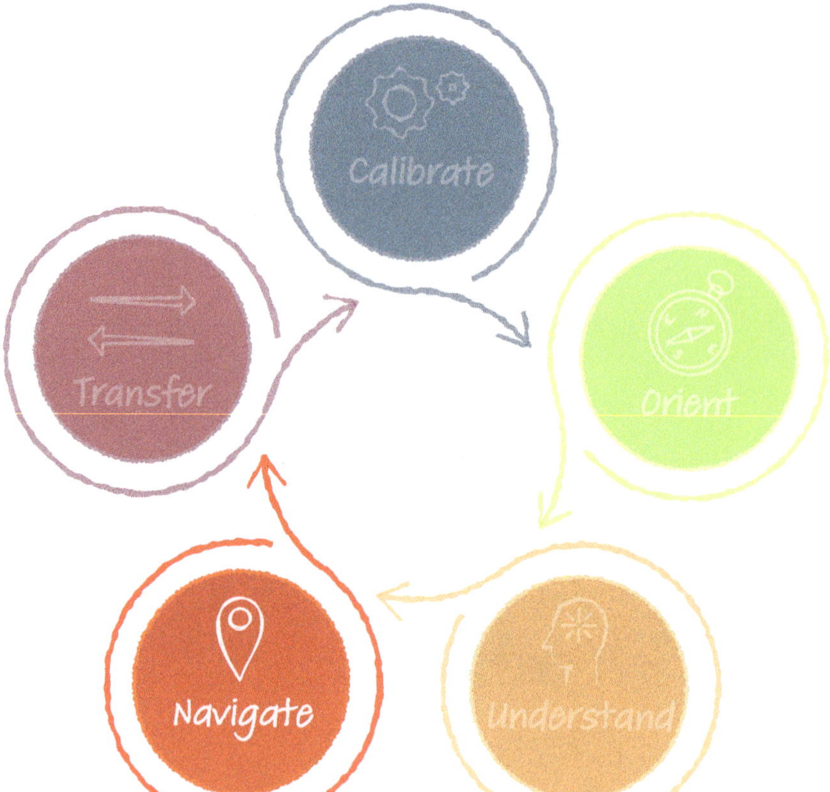
Calibrate
Orient
Understand
Navigate
Transfer

# CHAPTER SIX

# Navigate

*A smooth sea never made a skilled sailor.*

*– Franklin D. Roosevelt*

**Bracing to Stay Afloat**

The Northwest Territories of Canada is a beautiful, untamed and rugged landscape. In my late twenties, my husband wanted to realize his lifelong dream to canoe the Nahanni River. It is a wilderness river – one of the first to be declared a World Heritage site by the UN. Located about 500 kilometres west of the capital of Yellowknife, it is in quite a remote area in Arctic Canada. There are remarkable vistas throughout the entire Nahanni National Park Reserve, marked by diverse and expansive landscapes of mountain ranges, wide tundra plateaux, canyons, and Arctic forest. For paddling enthusiasts, the Nahanni River is the holy grail of canoe tripping. At the Virginia Falls, North America's most spectacular undeveloped waterfall, the river plunges into a series of four great canyons, where the walls rise over 4,000 feet, and the rapids are marked up to Class III difficulty.

As an experienced and confident swimmer but a novice overnight canoeist, it is an understatement to say I was nervous about making a trip recommended only for serious and practiced paddlers. My suggestion that we use the expertise and supervision of an experienced outfitting and guiding company with knowledge of the region went unheeded. But I wanted to support my husband's dream, so I agreed to embark on the adventure.

Along for the trip were two of his closest buddies. I was comforted by the knowledge that one was an experienced outdoorsman, and disquieted that our fourth canoeist was a dear, lanky, 6'5" friend who had a long-standing reputation as a lovable klutz with even less canoeing experience than me.

As we laboriously portaged our expedition-grade canoes around the Virginia Falls, the ground shook like a perpetual rumbling earthquake and the sky was filled with the sound of water crashing over 300 feet down and pounding the rocks in the canyon channel below. The volume of water rushing over the Virginia Falls, compressed into the narrow channels of the downstream river canyons, was a sight to behold. When we got to the foot of the falls, I was astonished to see that the whitewater seemed to rise 1-2 feet above the actual shoreline. My throat tightened at the thought of having to enter that raging torrent of a river.

There was real danger on this river. Not many travel the Nahanni as it is quite remote, and the terrain is rugged and unforgiving. Success requires a level of preparation, training and skill. The only other party we saw over two weeks and more than 165 miles on the river had trained and planned their trip for almost two years. We pulled our itinerary and equipment together in about six weeks. Seeing the boiling water crashing against the canyon walls and ancient boulders in its path made me deeply aware of how treacherous this river could be.

Somehow, we made it through those canyons, reaching our paddles out to brace our canoes and try to stay afloat. Our heavy-duty splash covers protected us from getting swamped by the roiling waves, but we were soaked nonetheless. Upstream of the falls, we could head towards an interesting vista and land the canoe for a hike up a scenic path. In that ferocious and challenging whitewater, the ability to choose our pace and direction disappeared.

We had absolutely no way to paddle, let alone steer a course. At this point in the river, my objective shifted to something far more basic and primal. Brace the canoe and don't sink. Don't hit the boulders and break the canoe or my head. Stay with the canoe at all costs, or I'll float away and drown. If we can all just hang on until the canyon widens up and relieves the pressure of the river, we'll come out the other end, more or less in one piece. Hopefully.

## Navigating Turbulence in Group Dynamics

In any meeting, be prepared to hit your own Nahanni moment, where your equipment, training and confidence will be tested. The meeting's objectives may be superseded. The agenda you hoped to follow will need to be tossed aside as you navigate unforeseen group dynamics. It may come in the form of disruptive people, a conflict that erupts in a session, factions or cliques forming, passive-aggressive behaviour, or some new information revealed that threatens to derail your conversation.

> *If the only tool you have in your tool kit is a hammer, then every problem looks like a nail.*

How do you handle a group that is unresponsive, disruptive or outright confrontational? What do you do when it feels like you're pushing limp spaghetti up a hill rather than leading a great, constructive discussion? Or when a few individuals show up as combative and get into conflict with each other or with you? What's the best strategy for handling well-intentioned individuals who are eager to contribute but tend to dominate the conversation or take it off track?

These are common examples of group dynamics that you have likely experienced. The way Conversation Leaders navigate them can make or break the meeting. There are common signs that you're about to get tossed off your surfboard and pitched into the lake. They include:

- Taking it personally and getting emotionally reactive in how you lead the discussion
- Listening more to your negative inner talk impedes you from being fully present for the group
- Feeling disrespected
- Fearing a loss of control, you try to reassert your authority over the group and switch from a collaborative and participatory decision-making framework to more of a top-down, command-and-control model of authority
- Shifting into blame, shame, justify instead of taking responsibility for what's happening in your conversation
- Ignoring the dynamic altogether, hoping that it will work itself out
- Feeling overwhelmed and abandoning the agenda or desired outcomes to go with the flow
- Shutting down the dynamic in a way that erodes psychological safety for the group
- Being unwilling to deviate from your game plan, widening the gap between what the group needs to do and how they are working together.

Up to this point, you've set the necessary foundations for having impactful and meaningful conversations. In Calibrate, you took steps to prepare yourself to be present, adaptive and confident in leading the discussion. In Orient, you stepped into the shoes of your participants and decided to start with their end in mind. In Understand, you learned the essential skills of listening well, communicating clearly and shifting perspective with intention so you can appreciate the various views and concerns that may arise. In Navigate, you'll learn what to do when group discussions get rocky.

## Encountering Team Toxins

Dr John Gottman, a relationship expert and best-selling author, identified specific toxic behaviours that come into play when relationships and discussions become combative and full of conflict. His framework of The Four Horsemen, or team toxins, shines a useful light on the dynamics that can undermine healthy relationships.

### *Criticism*

It's one thing to have a different perspective or priority, but when someone begins to criticize or blame someone's character instead of their contribution, you've just encountered the first Horseman. It can show up in aggressive attacks, a pattern of criticizing without offering alternatives, or someone who dominates more than contributes. Its arrival doesn't necessarily mean the relationship is broken, but unchecked blaming or critical behaviour disempowers and rejects the person on the receiving end and undermines the psychological safety and willingness to collaborate and work together in the group.

### Contempt

This toxin is a nasty amplification of criticism. Negative gossip, disrespect, demeaning behaviour or humour, sarcasm and even body language (think eye-rolling, scoffing, mimicking someone) are examples of contempt in action. Gottman's research indicated that contempt was the single biggest predictor of divorce in his studies of married couples. In a team meeting, contempt is like putting a drop of poison in the energy of connection and understanding you are working to create. It weakens the ability of the group to trust, respect and learn from each other. So much energy and focus must go into damage control outside the meeting, which decreases the group's productivity.

**Defensiveness**

Defensiveness is marked by deflection, excuses and not taking personal responsibility for your contribution to a problem. It often arises as a defence to criticism and leaves the person unwilling to shift their position or see new perspectives. Defensiveness can also devolve into placing blame and fault on others.

**Stonewalling**

In the face of contempt, individuals may respond by stonewalling behaviours. These include avoidance, disengagement, withholding, being uncooperative, and passivity. When facing a threat, the amygdala triggers a fight-flight-freeze response. Stonewalling encompasses the flight and freeze response. When an individual has been subjected to team toxins or brings other unresolved and stressful issues to the meeting table with them, their internal resourcefulness and ability to access their executive cognitive function are challenged. In a state of emotional overwhelm, they may not be able to think straight. It's best to take time out to allow the triggering brain hormones to ease and regain a sense of balance and the ability to re-engage in the discussion.

As the Conversation Leader, it's essential to know that when these team toxins show up, fixing them is not the responsibility of any particular individual. Toxins are a team issue. You are together as a collective system, operating as individuals within a web of connections, changing dynamics, varying opinions, different levels of expertise, and a range of communication styles and preferences.

What you do in those moments of stress is critical. Expect the unexpected. Those moments represent a turning point that can either strengthen or undermine the team. Some amount of stress or friction can be essential. After all, you can put all the right ingredients in the pan to bake a great cake, but if the oven isn't hot enough, you could end up with warm pudding instead.

> **A Framework for Feedback**
>
> When you encounter a team toxin in progress, address it before it derails or undermines your discussion. One helpful way to address a team toxin is to use a feedback method known as COIN, originally developed by Anna Carrol, MSW in 2003 (Mind Tools, 2018)
>
> **C – Context**
>
> Provide context for the issue or topic you want to address with the individual. Example: "I know that valuing and respecting people's contributions is important to us..."
>
> **O – Observation**
>
> State briefly a specific example of the behaviour you observed. Deliver it neutrally. Example: "I heard you make some negative statements about other team members..."

**I – Impact**

What is the impact of this behaviour on you, the group, the psychological safety of the conversation, or the organization? Be sure to frame it using "I" statements so you are not casting blame. Example: "When this happens, I feel it becomes unsafe to express a different point of view."

**N – Next Steps**

Make a specific request for the change you'd like to see and what you need from them instead. Deliver the request in a way that is encouraging and leave space to find a way to work more productively or effectively together. Example: "I request that if you have a criticism of an idea, you make it about the idea, not the person, and offer a constructive alternative. Are you willing to do this? How can we shift this dynamic so we as a team can feel respected and able to contribute freely to the discussion?"

Ideally, it's best to first deliver this feedback individually rather than in front of their peers, which may make them defensive. You can call a break and have a private conversation. Another way to handle this is to pause the group conversation and bring everyone back to the agreements and desired outcomes. Example: "Before we continue, I want to take a step back and have us all reconnect to our group agreements and why we are meeting. One agreement we've made is that we listen to understand and that if we disagree with a proposed solution, we need to offer an alternative. When we all do this, we get our best work done."

## Navigation Necessities

Navigating turbulence is a natural part of a group discussion, and three steps will help you stay on your toes and support the best outcome for the group: Step Back, Tune In and Speak Up.

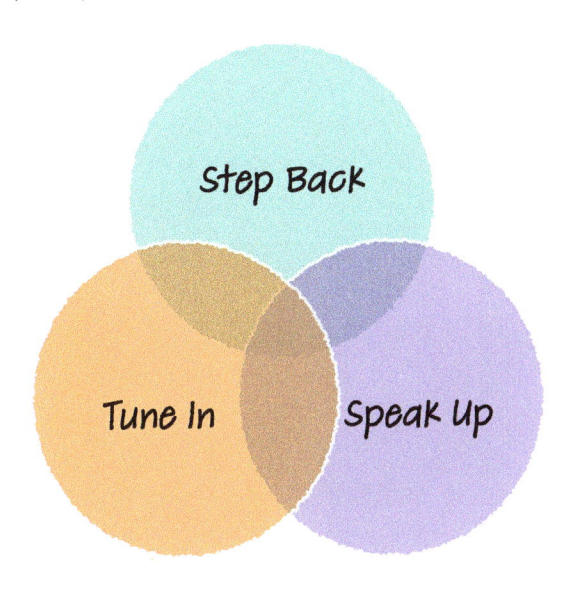

*Figure 7: Navigation Strategies*

### Step Back: Adjust Your Lens Strategically

***Look below the surface***

While teams are made up of individuals, each member is part of a dynamic, interdependent system. The person you think is missing the point may be suffering from being squeezed out of information flow and work by competitive colleagues trying to edge out a rising young millennial on the team. The person who is so quiet may be preoccupied, having learned that a colleague who will be quitting in two weeks asked them to keep it secret.

Instead of reacting to individuals as they show up in the room, stepping back allows you to pause and reflect on what might be happening at a broader, more systemic level. Zooming out to consider a bigger perspective enables you to notice group dynamics, patterns of behaviour and other signals that can yield important information about the group's needs.

Conflict or disconnection happens when there is some unexpressed need or perspective in play. If the Conversation Leader responds only to what's apparent, what's spoken and seems obvious without digging deeper into the heart of the matter, they will miss an important piece of what is really happening. You don't want to be like the Captain of the Titanic, paying attention only to what's above the waterline and oblivious to the scope of dangers below the surface. We all know that decision did not turn out well.

The good news is that you don't need to develop your extra-sensory perception to figure out why people are upset, uncooperative or disengaged. Understanding group dynamics is a bit like solving a puzzle. Every person brings their unique perspective, or piece, to the puzzle as a whole. Sometimes it may not be obvious how that piece fits in the big picture. But one thing is clear – your puzzle will have holes unless everyone puts their piece on the table.

It can be useful and illuminating to step back and see the bigger picture through a systems perspective. The iceberg model (Bryan et al, 2006; M. Goodman, 2002) shown in Figure 8 offers a simple tool you can use to discover root causes of events that may be more abstract and not immediately obvious. It has four levels as you move from what is seen and obvious, to what is generally unseen, abstract and harder to discern.

**THE ICEBERG**
*A Tool for Guiding Systemic Thinking*

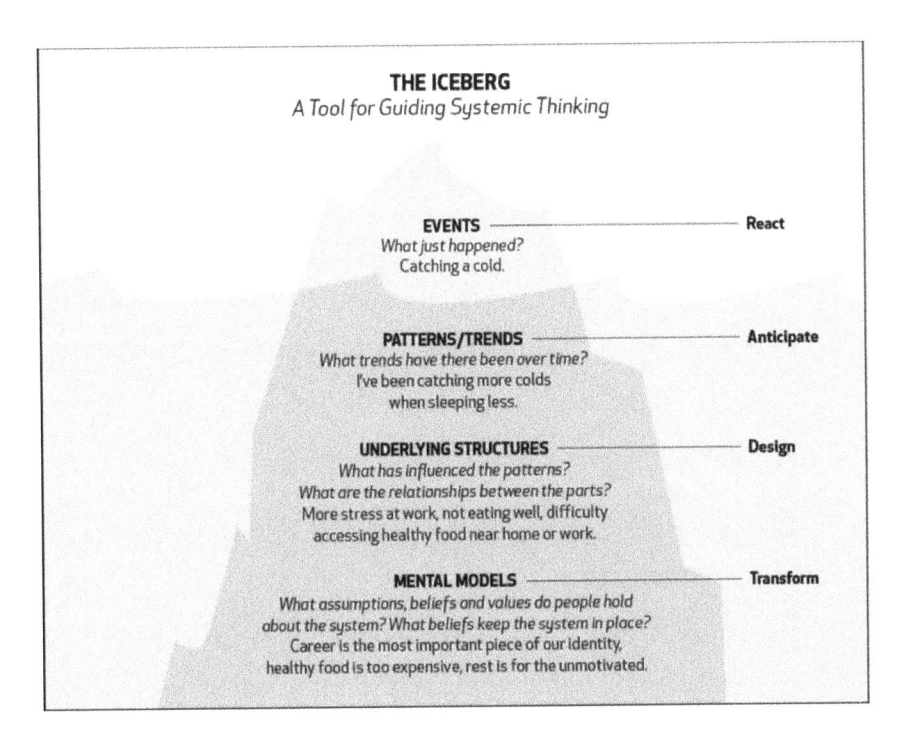

**EVENTS** — React
What just happened?
Catching a cold.

**PATTERNS/TRENDS** — Anticipate
What trends have there been over time?
I've been catching more colds
when sleeping less.

**UNDERLYING STRUCTURES** — Design
What has influenced the patterns?
What are the relationships between the parts?
More stress at work, not eating well, difficulty
accessing healthy food near home or work.

**MENTAL MODELS** — Transform
What assumptions, beliefs and values do people hold
about the system? What beliefs keep the system in place?
Career is the most important piece of our identity,
healthy food is too expensive, rest is for the unmotivated.

*Figure 8: The iceberg model of systemic thinking*
*(Image credit: https://www.nwei.org/iceberg)*

### *Events*

These are what you witness in a meeting, such as a comment, a behaviour, or an interaction where two people disagree. These are the immediate events that everyone can see. Did a person swear, or did they just muffle a sneeze? The question "What is happening right now?" helps clarify the dynamic so you can choose the appropriate response. Events cause us to react, but problems and conflicts will never be solved unless you dig into what created the event in the first place.

**Key question:** What is happening right now?

### Patterns/Trends

Going a level deeper, uncover how events may be connected to identify a pattern or trend. In your meeting, you anticipate that you might encounter these over time. Noticing that one person has been unusually quiet in recent discussions is a pattern. A series of missed deadlines on an important project is another. These patterns and trends offer clues to the event you witnessed. Adopting a systems perspective helps you to anticipate the patterns that give rise to events.

**Key questions:** What has been happening over time? What are the trends?

### Underlying Structures

At a deeper level of abstraction are the underlying structures that give rise to events, patterns and trends. This is where you may discover that the project's scope wasn't clear enough, and the lack of clarity is contributing to missed deadlines. The chronic stress of the pandemic and its impact on work/life balance could be another structure contributing to reduced patience and lower productivity. The inability of workers to access paid sick leave contributes to a decision to work even when feeling ill – a choice that has wide-ranging community consequences during a pandemic. By identifying structures that give rise to patterns and events, you can design solutions and create new structures that are better suited to your current needs.

**Key questions:** What's influencing these patterns? What are the connections between the patterns?

### Mental Models

At a root cause level, mental models describe the values and beliefs that hold the system in place. A mindset of how we do things around here, or that a new employee's perspective isn't as valid as someone more experienced, creates a ripple effect throughout the ecosystem of your organization.

**Key question:** What values, beliefs or assumptions shape the system?

### *Appreciate Different Perspectives*

It's essential to learn how to appreciate different perspectives. As much as we might wish it to be an objective state, reality can be experienced in many ways. It's like a kaleidoscope – even though it's the same physical object on the outside, the tumbling pieces of glass within are refracted in ever-changing and symmetrical patterns on mirrors. I might see a pattern of brilliant reds and yellows, but when I turn the kaleidoscope over to you, the shifts in weight and the tumbling glass pieces may arrange themselves into a configuration dominated by blues and greens. No pattern is the right one; they are just different, based on how we each held the kaleidoscope.

Appreciating varying perspectives helps build empathy and an ability to see the world through new eyes. We all have blind spots and biases, and encountering different views and perspectives illuminates them and shows where our assumptions may be holding us back.

In a workplace where we have workers from all different cultures, generations, faiths, ethnicities, sexual orientations and more, there is enormous value in seeking out and learning from different perspectives.

### *Put Everyone in the Same Boat*

As the saying goes, you're only as strong as your weakest link. Successful group discussion outcomes are the result of everyone's contributions. People always have something to offer; the question is whether it moves the group forward or is detrimental to progress.

It's important to have everyone in the same boat. When a problem arises, resist the temptation to jump in to address it or solve it right away. Ask group members for their input and response.

**Tune In: Communication is Crucial for Connection**

*Notice Signals from the System*

Have you ever walked into a room and sensed a whole lot of tension? Without hearing what has been said, you immediately know there's a chill in the air. You can pick this up in virtual spaces when someone appears held back or closed off, even in your limited view. They may turn off their camera for prolonged periods, despite your request to keep cameras on for the meeting.

Communication takes place in many forms and is a critical input in connecting and understanding one another. Bats operate through an incredible and sophisticated sonar system, where they fly using signals that bounce back from the environment around them. We, too, need to pay attention to signals. People communicate in many ways beyond just verbal. Listen to pauses, pace, tone and body language, as well as the words. Effective Conversation Leaders rely on what they hear and see and also on what they sense.

> Listen for what is NOT being said, as much as you listen for what IS being said.

When doing my graduate work at the Kennedy School at Harvard University in 1986, I had the privilege of taking a course called *Leadership and the Mobilization of Human Resources* with Professor Ron Heifetz, co-author of *The Practice of Adaptive Leadership*. The course had a fascinating structure with twice-weekly classes that were very active discussions between the professor and students. The course addressed significant, contentious topics, such as racism, discrimination, social and economic injustice, and more. In our weekly small group discussions, we had to present a mini case study of our personal leadership failures and, with the help of the small group, link it back to the teachings and themes that emerged in the large lecture class.

In one lecture, we discussed the impact of apartheid in South Africa, a system of segregationist policies against non-whites that was still in place in the late 1980s. Students in the class came from countries from all over the world, and many were of African-American descent. At one point, a white male South African student rose up to hotly defend apartheid. He proceeded to storm out of the lecture hall while many students implored him to stay and discuss this important issue.

During this incident, I noticed I was having a strong physical reaction. It wasn't the first time I had felt this way in this class. My face flushed, my throat tightened, and my palms began to sweat. A question was formulating in my mind, but my inner critic shut it down. What if I asked a stupid question? That would be embarrassing, so better not do that. Perhaps I'd missed something, and my question had already been answered. Whether it was my identity as an extremely polite and compliant Canadian or my overwhelm and disbelief at the good fortune of doing my graduate work at such a prestigious university, my imposter syndrome was pretty adept at censoring me.

As if he had read my mind, Professor Heifetz stopped to ask if anyone in the class felt like their body was resonating. I hadn't heard the word used much at that time, but it certainly described what I was feeling. I knew he was also an accomplished cellist, so perhaps the word "resonate" was a regular part of his vocabulary. He urged, "If you feel something in your body that needs to be said, you should speak it. Sometimes we resonate when others in the system need to be heard, and you can be a voice for that need." It was the first time I was given a vocabulary for understanding that we may think we operate independently from one another, but when we gather in collective intention, a system of collective intelligence begins to form and can take on a life of its own.

Masterful Conversation Leaders learn to cultivate and incorporate their own gut-sensing sonar, so you notice it when you get a "ping". Pay attention to the internal signals and nudges you receive when you relax and tune in to your whole-body intelligence, not just your intellect. Don't try to analyze it right away with your brain or through the filters of past experience, but instead stay open and curious. I now call it my "spidey sense," and it's a nudge that I have learned to trust so I can tune deeply into what is really happening. It may not always be 100 percent accurate, but at the very least, use it to prompt a clarifying question. Get curious about what may be happening beneath the events taking place on the surface of your conversation.

**Question Your Assumptions**

Everyone has a blind spot where we don't know what we don't know. Our expertise and experience can keep us blinkered to new perspectives and solutions. We need to rely on others to show ideas and patterns that we just can't see. Under stress, blind spots can get even bigger, so it's important to question your assumptions. That person you assume is being difficult by questioning the direction of the discussion may, in fact, be courageous, taking a risk to express a concern felt by many in the group.

> "Begin challenging your own assumptions. Your assumptions are your windows on the world. Scrub them off every once in a while, or the light won't come in."
>
> – *Alan Alda*

It's hard to solve problems because everyone has a different perspective, or there isn't a common understanding of what the situation entails. Rather than assume, it's best to review and check for common understanding as part of your work context. When operating in so much uncertainty, we can't take anything for granted.

Many Conversation Leaders fall into the trap of responding to participants in a piecemeal or personal approach. "Oh, that person is always missing the point" or "I wish that person wouldn't be so quiet. Don't they care about this?" are often judgments when individuals aren't meeting your expectations.

Stay in the present moment – that is where the magic happens. Like alchemists turning lead to gold, meaningful conversations where people listen and share honestly with each other can turn challenges into unforeseen and unexpected opportunities.

### Shift From the Dance Floor to the Balcony

At university, I played volleyball. To score a point when playing offense, you have two choices: use brute strength to strike the ball so hard the other team can't control the ball and return it, or find a hole in their defence and direct the ball there. Directing the volleyball to score a point requires finesse and accuracy, not just an ability to jump high and hit hard. When watching other teams play from the stands, it was easy enough to see when a team left its sideline open for a spike down the line, or if a particular defender was out of position and left a gap in the mid-court. But when you're on the court, in the action, it's not so easy to spot the holes.

A key skill in the framework of adaptive leadership is getting off the dance floor and going to the balcony (Heifetz & Linsky, 2009). At some point, as the Conversation Leader, you need to step away from the back and forth discussion and observe the dynamics from a more global vantage point. By shifting between the balcony perspective and the dance floor, you learn to inhabit the observer and participant's role at the same time. "Leadership is an improvisational art," says Heifetz. "You may be guided by an overarching vision, clear values, and a strategic plan, but what you actually do from moment to moment cannot be scripted. You must respond as events unfold." (Heifetz & Linsky, 2002). One person you must also witness from the balcony is yourself and how you are showing up on the dance floor. The mindset of curiosity and humility that you adopted in the Calibrate phase will support your ability to self-reflect, assess, and make new choices in an instant.

## Speak Up: Hold the Space

I was introduced to the concept of "holding the space" when attending my first shadow work transformational seminar in California. It seemed very important for the people running this three-day immersive experience, but I took it very literally. "How can you hold space?" I wondered. "Space isn't something you can touch or hold. It's invisible."

As I continued in my coaching training and started to assist and mentor people going through transformational intensives, often highly charged and emotional experiences, I realized the importance of the concept of space in providing a safe environment in which people can work. In my assisting days, holding the space wasn't just about listening and supporting people. It included thinking about arranging the chair and the assistants physically around the room to provide a calming and supportive presence just by sitting there.

Creating the appropriate space for your conversation is like planting a garden. There is an entire ecosystem to consider that is ever-changing, and you need to be responsive to those changes. Select the best location, and notice how much sunlight it gets. Prepare the ground by removing rocks and weeds, then work the soil and add mulch or other amendments to hold water. When the soil is ready, you plant the seeds to the right depth. Your garden requires constant care to water and fertilize it, pull out weeds, and prune back the plants to remove parts that are no longer viable and are taxing the root system. You might find you need to build a fence around the garden, to keep out critters that want to nibble tender plant shoots as they emerge from the ground. But a garden isn't all about the work of planting and tending. It's also about taking a step back to appreciate its beauty, to marvel at how it changes over the seasons, and to bring its bounty out into the world, perhaps through a bouquet of flowers or learning how to make a tasty zucchini bread from your vegetable patch.

### *Name It to Tame It*

One important role you play in leading the conversation is to notice and speak to the dynamics witnessed in the group. There is nothing more distracting than the elephant in the room. It could be a simple acknowledgement of the stress everyone must be feeling juggling working from home with children attending school virtually. You may need to call out conflicts between colleagues with a simple, "I notice there's some friction happening here. Is there something you'd like to share so we can support you?" If something is happening that might be taking you out of being fully present, then name that too. "I'm a bit nervous because I want to use a new online tool in our meeting today, so I ask for your patience as I go up a learning curve with it."

Emerging Conversation Leaders often hold back from naming dynamics because they feel they have to solve it, even when they are uncomfortable or unsure what to do. Ignoring issues erodes the quality of the space and the trust people have in you to lead the conversation well. If you reflect on what you observe and create an opportunity for a discussion, then everyone is invited to share ownership for how to address it.

### Use the Grit

As the Conversation Leader, you must take the stance that there is wisdom waiting to be discovered in any conflict or difficult moment. Few of us are naturally comfortable dealing with conflict, and managing these situations is one of the greatest challenges a leader faces. As Ron Heifetz says, "Conflict is a necessary part of the change process and, if handled properly, can serve the engine of progress." (Heifetz & Linsky, 2002).

Use moments of conflict as an opportunity to go deeper. The oyster cannot create its pearl without a single piece of grit to start the process. The oyster secretes a fluid to soothe the grit's irritation, and layers of that secretion form the pearl. Dial up your curiosity and dial down snap judgments. Bring it to the group's awareness and ask, "What else is happening here that we need to see now?"

If you consider your group as a system rather than a collection of individuals, you can view conflict as a voice of the system; offering feedback is expressing an unmet need. Rather than viewing conflict as wrong, a mistake or a reflection on your management of the discussion, a systemic view offers that conflict helps the system reveal itself to itself. Greater awareness of the group brings new information and perspectives, which can be leveraged to turn the grit into a pearl.

### Create Psychological Safety

For teams to contribute their best and be their best, people need to feel safe to express themselves. To do this requires psychological safety, a term first coined by Harvard Professor Amy Edmondson, author of *The Fearless Organization*. She defines psychological safety as "a belief that one will not be punished or humiliated for speaking up with ideas, questions, concerns or mistakes." (Edmondson, 2019). This means you feel free to ask questions and share ideas without fear that you will be judged, pounced upon in a "gotcha" moment, or dismissed.

Consider the broader context of living and working in the COVID-19 pandemic era, where we each navigate the chronic stress and fear of the virus itself and the changing public health rules that impact us on a daily level. Here, our brains are regularly operating at a fairly high level of alert for potential danger.

When there's psychological safety, people feel connected to each other and to the purpose of their work together. In *Daring Greatly*, Brené Brown defines connection as "the energy that exists between people when they feel seen, heard, and valued; when they can give and receive without judgment; and when they derive sustenance and strength from the relationship." (Brown, 2015).

Like an electrical system, if a wire is disconnected or too many appliances are switched on to an old circuit, you may blow a fuse and lose all power. Unaddressed team toxins trip the circuits on how your group connects. Simply side-stepping moments of conflict or shutting them down entirely so the group can get back on track squanders the opportunity to potentially strengthen and sustain the connection you want to have in the group. Connection in a group is crucial, and it is only possible when you feel a level of psychological safety.

> *Psychological safety at work takes effort.*
> *It's not the norm. But it's worth the effort.*
>
> *– Amy Edmondson*

### Tips for Virtual Conversations

When things get rocky in a virtual meeting – and they will, from time to time – you need to know how to manage the situation. Conflict, challenging statements, or a sudden prolonged silence do not mean that something has gone wildly off the rails. But there are some dynamics that you can manage to unearth the gifts that conflict can bring to a group's awareness, and ensure that the technology isn't working counter to your goal of leading Conversations that Count.

### 💡 Earn People's Attention

You might have noticed that attention spans are shorter than ever and distractions are higher than ever. When working remotely, everything is pinging us – notifications and emails from our screens, and dogs and children clamouring for attention. The struggle to stay focused and on-task is real. We're constantly managing the temptation to go and check something else – rather than keeping our focus on that virtual meeting.

Consider that you need to earn every moment of attention from your participants. You don't just deserve it just because someone works for you. To build relationships and get the most from people, we need to step it up a notch. Mark Bowden, body language and communication expert, says our brains have a window of engagement of about 15-20 minutes. "Create surprise, variety and texture by building your presentation with smaller pieces of content," he advises (Bowden, 2021). Break your meeting into bite-sized chunks, and give people the opportunity to digest those chunks through asking questions, having more in-depth breakout discussions, or even doing some personal reflection and writing in the chatbox.

### 💡 Skillful Screen Sharing

Be mindful of what your participants see on screen. If you put up a few introductory slides then forget to remove screen-share while discussing the content, people start to lose connection with each other. If you're having a discussion, make it a protocol that you'll then go back to speaker view or even gallery view. Remind people how to manage their virtual real estate between gallery view and speaker view so they don't zone out.

How you manage what people view on-screen impacts their energy, sense of connection, and engagement. For example, I recently attended my high school reunion – an event we hold every five years with people attending from all over the world. During the pandemic, this eagerly awaited ritual couldn't happen in person, so the school arranged a virtual reunion. It provided an opportunity to connect with other graduating classes five years on either side of us.

My classmates gathered virtually from around the world, excited to reconnect. We were met with a screen share of a slide show of historical photos of the school, which was nice to see. However, the screen share meant that new arrivals showed up as a small thumbnail photo in the gallery group. The excitement and enthusiasm quickly started to drop as we couldn't readily find our classmates. Nor could we see people from other years to wave or send a quick chat to.

After a few minutes, I asked the event organizer to stop sharing the screen so we could have a full gallery view of everyone. Once they did so, there was a huge and immediate surge of energy in the room. People got excited, with cross talk, spontaneous shout outs and greetings as we welcomed each other. It really helped to foster connection and restored the delight we have come to experience at our reunions.

If someone is managing your screen, be clear when you want them to share a screen, pin someone's video, or bring the group back to the gallery view.

### 💡 Make Conversation Visible

Sometimes things get heated in a meeting because people simply aren't understanding each other anymore. If you rely too much on verbal communication, it's hard to determine whether there is consensus on assumptions or what words mean. For example, in my divorce settlement, I negotiated the right to use our summer cottage for three weeks with our children for a period of five years after the divorce. After everything was signed and sealed, I was surprised when my ex advised me he didn't consider the week to include weekends, which effectively granted me access to the property only from Monday to Friday. Versions of this kind of misunderstanding, intentional or not, can lead to friction and an erosion of trust and effectiveness.

One way to mitigate the risk of misunderstandings is to make the conversation visible. Doing so can clarify group discussion because it shifts the dynamic of people butting heads with each other to one where they are more shoulder-to-shoulder. Use the tools that are built into most videoconferencing platforms, like the chatbox or annotation tools. You can also use external tools to support collaborative decision-making processes. Sticky notes, flipcharts, visual frameworks and maps help people to see the big picture. Jamboard, Slido, Google docs, Mural, and Miro are just a few of the online collaborative tools I've used to help groups do brainstorming and decision-making processes.

For some meetings, you may want to bring in a trained facilitator or a digital graphic recorder to help structure the agenda and visually document your discussions in a way that enlivens and supports participant engagement. Graphic recording is an impactful and invaluable sense-making tool. In this process, graphic recorders (also known as scribes or visual facilitators) listen for key ideas, themes and issues and capture them visually in real-time during a discussion. This can be done for in-person meetings on large foam core boards or paper with markers or drawing apps and an iPad in virtual meetings. It allows everyone to be on the same page – because the page is created based on the group discussion and unfolds visually before the group in real-time.

## Take Action

```
NAVIGATE INGREDIENTS

More of:                              Less of:
☑ Go below the surface                ☒ Take things personally
☑ Put everyone in the same            ☒ Ignore team toxins
  boat                                ☒ Stay at the surface
☑ Notice and respond to               ☒ Be right and stay
  signals                               comfortable
☑ Question your assumptions           ☒ Treat people differently
☑ Go from dance floor to the          ☒ Be oblivious to signals
  balcony                             ☒ Ignore the elephant in the
☑ Name it to tame it                    room
☑ Conflict as grit

Add Your Own Ingredients:             Watch Out For:
_____               _____
_____               _____
_____               _____
```

### ✓ Your Experience of Team Toxins

Review the team toxins and think back to meetings you've attended – either as the Conversation Leader or as a participant – where you experienced them in action. You might also have noticed examples in relationships outside the office.

For each team toxin, consider what it looked, sounded and felt like when this behaviour was being demonstrated. What solution or antidote would you use when you encounter this same dynamic in future?

| TEAM TOXINS | What it LOOKED like | What it SOUNDED like | How it FELT to you | Potential Solutions and Antidotes |
|---|---|---|---|---|
| Criticism | | | | |
| Contempt | | | | |
| Defensiveness | | | | |
| Stonewalling | | | | |

### ✅ Transform Grit into a Pearl

Develop a practice of using conflict as the potential for some constructive purpose. Note your responses to these questions to help transform the grit into a pearl.

**What is the grit?** Describe the incident or interaction that you found challenging or difficult.

_____
_____
_____
_____

**What is the irritation?** Why did this incident bother you? Answer this question from the perspective of being on the dance floor. Notice any thoughts, feelings, beliefs or disempowering stories it may have stirred up. How did this irritation impact you?

_____

_____

_____

_____

**Shift your perspective.** Now imagine stepping off the dance floor and up to the balcony. Replay this conflict in your mind as an observer. What other impacts did you see this incident have on the group? What dynamics, changes in participation, or energy shifted?

_____

_____

_____

_____

**Find the pearl.** Take a deep breath and ask what the potential gift in this conflict is. If conflict is a voice of the system, what unmet needs are being expressed? How could this be useful and support the group in its work together? Perhaps it's an opportunity to clarify values or priorities or help people who are feeling disconnected or stressed?

_____

_____

**Make a choice.** What decision can you make now that will use this incident as a catalyst to support your group's work?

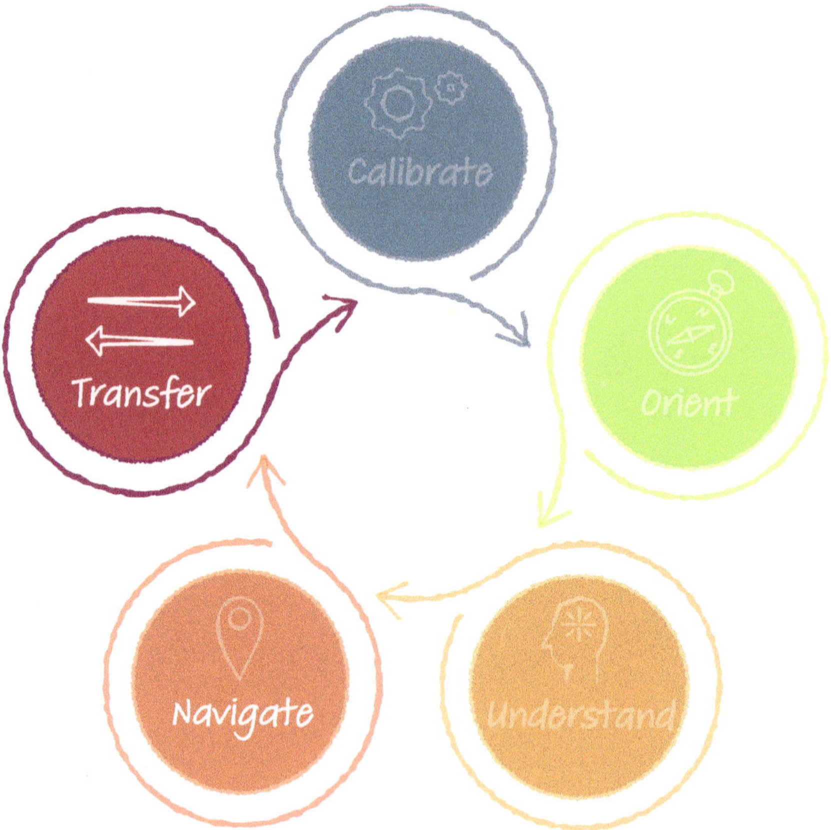
Calibrate
Orient
Understand
Navigate
Transfer

# CHAPTER SEVEN

# Transfer

*Most organizations act as if naming the problem and articulating the solution are enough.*

– *Dr Ron Heifetz*

## Break the Board

I learned an important life lesson when I joined a self-defence class for women. As a single professional woman who occasionally had to work late at night in a large city, I decided I would feel more peace of mind if I knew some self-defence basics. Over the one-day workshop, I learned the best stance to keep my balance if confronted, how to break the grip of someone trying to grab me, and the vulnerable points to aim for if faced with an attacker.

The final task of the workshop was to break a wooden board with my bare fist. As my fellow participants and I dubiously handed out the boards to each other, we all looked skeptical. These boards were solid and heavy. I didn't want to break a bone. The instructor shared a key tip on how to break the board successfully, without injuring your hand in the process. "To break the board, you'll need to use a lot of force as you bring your hand down. But don't make the mistake of stopping the force when you contact the surface of the board, otherwise, you will hurt your hand," she cautioned. "Instead, visualize a point an inch or two below the board and bring your force down to that point. If you do that, you'll be able to break the board easily, and you won't feel a thing."

After psyching myself up, I followed her instruction and was amazed that not only did I break the board in my first attempt, but that my hand didn't hurt at all. You might think, sure, that's easy enough to do with a regular 2x4 board. But years later, I witnessed my son-in-law apply the same principle (with considerably more skill and confidence) in breaking three concrete blocks stacked on top of each other – with his bare hand. It was an incredible feat to witness, and my palms still sweat just thinking about it.

## Drive Through the Finish Line, Not Just To It

Breaking a board and running a successful meeting have something in common. To break the board, you need to direct your energy and momentum past the surface to a point behind it. You focus on a goal beyond what is visible and direct your energy through to that place.

The same is true in a meeting. The purpose of a meeting isn't just to have one. Transfer is about taking the energy from the meeting conversation and bringing it out into the workplace in some tangible and measurable way. The meeting is a means to an end for accomplishing a set of specific objectives. Whether the work is solving a problem, launching a product, or setting new priorities, the conversation is in service of something being different from the status quo. Leading a Conversation that Counts includes the crucial step of considering how you support the group to transfer the collective decisions and momentum of the meetings into tangible next steps.

## The meeting isn't over when the meeting is over. It's over when the work gets done.

Bringing a group of people together in one room for an important discussion is a significant investment for your organization. If you add up the billable hours of people's time, travel, accommodation, room charges, food and beverages, you're looking at a hefty price tag. Even though meeting virtually does remove some of the hard costs from the equation, the virtual room is costly because your battle for your attendee's attention and participation is different in an environment rich with distractions, like the temptation to multi-task, handle barking dogs or hungry children, or the siren call of one's email inbox.

Consider the risk if all the insights and excitement about the next steps fizzle as soon as people leave. What is the cost when your people click out of the virtual meeting in a haze, suffering from Zoom fatigue? How costly is ineffective action? How much goodwill, commitment, and innovation do you lose when your teams suffer from change fatigue?

In 1885, the scientist Hermann Ebbinghaus described the ability of the brain to retain memory over time. Known as the "Forgetting Curve," the speed with which we forget learned knowledge over time is astonishing (Wikipedia, 2021). Cognitive science expert Art Kohn says we forget approximately 50 percent of new information within an hour and an average of 70 percent within a day. After a week, the average loss goes up to 90 percent (Chartwell Content, 2017).

Of course, some moments are seared into our memories forever, like the birth of a child or remembering exactly where you were when you heard about the 9/11 attacks. Nonetheless, if you think about the content of the meetings we attend, who said what when, and what we committed to do at the end, it can all become a big blur.

Solving big problems and making great plans is one thing, but we must carry through on that commitment and allow time to make it specific, actionable and memorable. How do you keep the goodwill, momentum and positive intention you've created in your conversation and translate that into action? In this chapter, you'll learn how to do just that.

## Walking the Talk

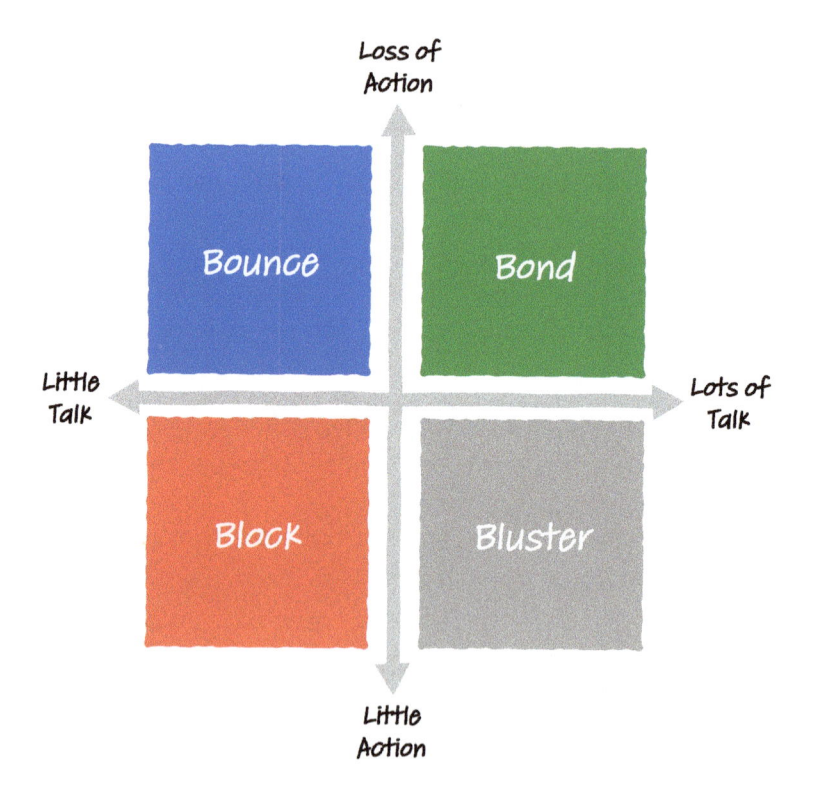

*Figure 9: Effective Meetings Matrix*

One of the best indicators of whether the conversation will lead to tangible results is the alignment between talk and action. In Figure 9, you can see which category of meetings you've had, based on the proportion of talk and action.

**Block: Little Talk and Little Action**

Meetings characterized by little talk and minimal action-taking are a key driver of change fatigue and cynicism. These kinds of conversations are typically informational sessions, where the person hosting the meeting does all the talking, leaving little space for others to speak or offer contrary views, and no focus on defining and assigning next steps. This meeting feels more like a "show and tell" experience than a conversation that counts. Participants are simply a passive audience, forced to show up and watch someone else's show.

**Bluster: Lots of Talk and Little Action**

We've all been in meetings with plenty of rhetoric and lots of promises, but where nothing really happens. This can be more engaging if the meeting leader delivers with greater energy. But when nothing meaningful changes after the rah-rah exhortations, the resulting skepticism and cynicism becomes a drag on productivity and engagement in future sessions. Town Hall sessions, designed to communicate strategic information and inspire the workforce, can fall into this trap.

I worked with the same client for several years at their global senior leadership retreat. Each year I heard the same key messages about the importance of building a vibrant and unified culture and creating psychological safety to encourage diversity of thought in support of their diversity, equity and inclusion initiatives. It felt like these gatherings had become a "Groundhog Day" experience. Each year brought the same message because the expressed need for change was not meaningfully embedded in the company's day-to-day operational and relationship fabric.

## Bounce: Little Talk and Lots of Action

This conversation is where every meeting feels like you're bouncing into a new scene of a different movie. It might happen in an organization experiencing a lot of change or shifts in leadership roles and where there is little consistency. It can also result from a disorganized and overly enthusiastic group leader who wants to try out the latest musings on team development and project management on the group.

I sometimes call this the "throw spaghetti at the wall and see what sticks" approach to managing a group. There isn't sufficient designed conversation to elicit ideas from the group. The leaders of Bounce conversations are often concerned about being seen as doing something but uncertain how to discern the most important next step. People invest their time and energy in meetings, and when there is no connection or through-line from one meeting to the next, they get cynical. Why did they bother to give their ideas if there is no follow-up from the last meeting?

A new department head presented a document on a new direction she envisioned for her unit. She had prepared it alone and brought it to the team meeting. There was plenty of discussion and confusion about the lack of participation in its creation and the short timeframe for input. Shortly after the initial conversations, she submitted the document to the senior executive for final approval. When asked how committed her team was to this new vision for the department, she sincerely told the COO that she had conducted consultation and everyone had thoroughly vetted and approved the direction.

Some six months later, the Director of HR reported workplace complaints arising from the department. In the view of some staff, the new direction impacted existing job responsibilities and reporting relationships, and employees felt there had not been due process in implementing the change. They perceived the proposal around departmental change was handled as a "one and done" presentation and felt the only way their voices could be heard was by lodging formal complaints through HR. It became clear that while the new Department head had technically scheduled group discussion and input, there had been insufficient time and effort put into winning the hearts and minds of the people directly affected by the proposed changes.

**Bond: Lots of Talk and Lots of Action**

When you lead a conversation that balances the need to include participants' perspectives and keep a shared, collective focus on driving clear outcomes, you create a bond. Engaged participants who are supported through a shared focus have a conversation where people understand their role as individuals in contributing to the overall picture.

When actions back up the commitments and ideas discussed, there's an undeniable sense of momentum and trust. You truly feel you can count on each other. A wonderful example is an oft-told story of President John F. Kennedy's visit to NASA headquarters in 1961. While touring the facilities, Kennedy chatted with a janitor mopping the floor and asked him what he did. The janitor's reply demonstrated the strong bond and purpose he felt in his job when he answered, "I'm helping put a man on the moon!"

## Transfer Strategies

You have invested a lot of your energy and time to lead a conversation that builds goodwill, clarity and connection. You've moved the ball down the field, but you aren't across the finish line until you transfer the momentum from that meeting into tangible action and change.

You still need to ensure the ideas and understandings you've created in your conversation don't dissipate once people leave the meeting or Zoom room. Three areas will ensure that you transfer all that talk into meaningful result: Action, Alignment, and Accountability

*Figure 10: Transfer Strategies*

## Action: Imperfect Action is Better than Perfect Inaction

One of the biggest mistakes I've seen is creating an agenda that doesn't allow enough time or mental bandwidth to consider the next steps. Without attention and planning for action steps, the impact of your conversation will evaporate shortly after its conclusion. Unless you transfer the clarity and decisions into the day-to-day reality, it becomes just one more piece of information that burdens your cognitive load.

To get focused on action-taking, ask, what will be different tomorrow? Who is taking responsibility for which actions, and when does that work need to be completed? Talking about developing a resilient culture is great, but what will that look like? How will people interact and engage with clients or each other? How does that impact the processes and systems in place? What do you need to do more, start doing, or stop doing?

Don't just talk; take action. Often the best way to figure something out is to take one single step. Choose something and move. See what works and build from there. Appreciate what didn't work and let it go.

> *A baby step, taken consistently, is more impactful than a giant leap now and then.*

Focus on taking action instead of making everything perfect. Set it up as an experiment to see what works and what didn't. Mistakes only indicate a failure when you repeat them, not when you learn from them. Inertia and analysis paralysis suck the energy out of teams. Don't try to shoehorn in discussions about implementation and priority-setting at the end of a crammed agenda. Design opportunities to keep that end in mind right from the start of your meeting.

**Alignment: Build in Structures to Support Ongoing Alignment**

As a tall person prone to occasional flare-ups of lower back and neck pain, I make regular trips to my chiropractor to adjust my spine. It always amazes me that the source of a particular pain is often not adjacent to where I experience the knot of tension. One little spot of misalignment creates ripple effects throughout my body. My foot out of alignment puts pressure on other parts to compensate for not balancing properly, and before you know it, I have a knot in my shoulder. Maintenance visits keep me flexible and pain-free.

Teams get out of alignment when they lack clarity about the decision they are asked to make. It's essential to be upfront about whether their input is for information-sharing, brainstorming, or actual decision-making. Part of your role as the Conversation Leader is to share your expectations with the group. Don't confuse people's attendance with acceptance. Silence doesn't mean people agree with what is being discussed. When you treat group discussions about important issues as an activity to simply check the box on (as the Department head did in the earlier example), you'll run into problems in implementing and executing your objectives.

Many years ago, I worked with a company that had experienced huge growth through acquisition, resulting in a mosaic of different subcultures within the company. They wanted to create more alignment and shared understanding of their mission and values, so they expended a lot of time and energy in senior leadership offsites to talk about the importance of using their values of respect, learning and continuous improvement to navigate some of the integration issues and business challenges they faced. It all sounded very inspirational, coming from the stage at the annual leadership retreat. Yet as I worked with that client over a number of years, I kept hearing the same messages shared repeatedly. "Work together as one." "Respect each other and leverage our strengths," and "Together, we deliver great value to our customers." I wondered if those leaders felt like Bill Murray in the movie *Groundhog Day*, where the main character keeps waking up and reliving the same day over and over again until he finally gets it right in the end (Groundhog Day, 1993).

How do you embed lofty ideals and values into tangible, gritty, step-by-step actions on a day-to-day basis? How do you walk your talk with each other? What agreements can you create to support building alignment in the trenches of the daily work, and not just in the retreat center at your offsite?

The Conversation Leader must design for and address alignment upfront in the meeting. As organizational psychologist and author, Roger Schwartz, says, "If even one person in your meeting doesn't know how they are supposed to contribute to the meeting, you increase the risk that they will get the meeting off track." Help participants get clear about their role in the meeting. You can indicate this before the meeting starts through the agenda and any pre-meeting work you ask them to do. As Schwartz says, "If it's your meeting, and you don't tell people the roles you expect them to play, and then they act at odds with your expectations, you've helped create the problem." (Schwartz, 2016).

**Accountability: Take Responsibility for Your Actions**

It's unfortunate when the "Next Steps" section of a meeting receive a perfunctory 15 minutes at the end of a long day, when people's energy, focus and willpower are likely at a low point. Frame the importance of taking clear action at the start of your conversation. Powerful questions you can ask include:

- What's next?
- So what? Why does this matter?
- What's going to be different tomorrow morning as a result of this?
- Who is going to do what, and by when?

Just as the janitor at the Kennedy Space Center told President Kennedy his job was to help put a man on the moon, people need sight lines to understand how they fit in and contribute to the big picture. This provides a sense of intrinsic motivation and a connection to why their work matters.

Create a flexible structure that allows for the unexpected and is strong enough to keep you together when the going gets tough. Plan for regular communication between meetings, so the information flow is transparent, relevant and timely. Whether by email, internal instant messaging system or other means, agree on how best to keep in touch so you can have a running start at your next meeting, rather than spending a chunk of it recapping or re-orienting people to issues already discussed. Designate a weekly planning standup meeting to focus on what needs to be accomplished in the week ahead. Use these channels to report and share new information, insights and challenges.

Use visual tools, such as dashboards, Gantt charts, or graphic recordings, to help the team see how everyone is progressing and keep clear on who is responsible for what. Find ways to keep the big picture in mind so folks don't get lost in the weeds in between meetings.

## Visual Tools Provide a Roadmap

"A picture says a thousand words" is certainly true when finding ways to visualize your conversation. From graphic recording to journey maps to a RACI matrix, many visual tools can help ensure your decisions and priorities are transferred into meaningful action after the conversation ends.

I am a strong proponent of making conversation visual because it helps make the invisible visible. When people are in conflict, they butt heads together. But when you put your ideas up on sticky notes to complement their verbal expression or bring in a trained visual facilitator to support drawing out your conversation in real-time, something profound happens. With visual tools, you collectively make a map of your thinking which makes it easier to see connections and synergies. Potential gaps and obstacles become more apparent, and the dynamic shifts from butting heads to being shoulder-to-shoulder as you make sense of the map you created together.

Beyond this important shift in helping the team work and see the big picture together, visual artifacts provide a roadmap to direct your team's actions during and after the meeting. They are an ongoing reference tool to keep people aligned and make it easy to celebrate progress, and notice where the work may have veered off the path. Making your work visual makes it easier to answer the question "Are we there yet?" and determine what else needs to be put in place so you can answer that question with a resounding "Yes, we did it!"

## Tips for Virtual Conversations

Ending a virtual meeting requires just a click of the button on the part of your participants, not unlike the action they take when they've finished binge-watching the latest season of their favourite show on Netflix. Except at the end of a meeting, they need to be motivated to take action and be clear on who is going to do what. Try some of the following ideas to ensure that momentum is successfully transferred into clear action and execution.

### 💡 Don't Be Afraid to Go "Old school"

Even though there are myriad options for cool tech tools and ways to communicate online, sometimes there's nothing like good old pen and paper to help with retention and recall. Encourage your participants to jot down some notes during the meeting to improve their retention and understanding of the discussion. Studies show that students who write longhand notes remembered more and had a more comprehensive understanding of the material presented (May, 2014).

Instead of waiting for the usual to-do list to appear after the meeting courtesy of a designated notetaker, ask participants to write down their next action step on a sticky note, hold it to the camera and take a screenshot of everyone with their next steps. Send that picture out as part of the meeting report as a visually interesting and memorable artifact to your group. Participants can then post their sticky note to their computer as a visual reminder of the action step they committed to.

### 💡 Stay Behind After the Meeting

It's important to start and end meetings on time as a way to respect and honor people's busy schedules. However, as the meeting host, you don't necessarily want to pounce on the "End meeting for all" button as soon as the meeting is scheduled to end. You've likely had the experience with in-person sessions where someone would want to hang back to raise a question with you outside of the official group meeting. Or perhaps you've been the one who hung around at the end to share something or ask a question you felt was too sensitive to raise in front of the group.

We've lost that opportunity for informal and important intelligence gathering and connection at the beginning and end of our virtual meetings. Let people know you'll stay on the videoconference for another ten minutes if anyone wants to talk. It's an extra opportunity to build connection and learn what's going on for people. Chances are that no one will take you up on that invitation to linger, but they'll likely appreciate your availability. And if they do stick around to have that more personal discussion with you, it's likely to be informative for how you lead your next meeting.

### 💡 Ask for Feedback

Despite the ups and downs of living and working through a global pandemic, we're still on a learning curve in creating impactful and meaningful Conversations that Count. Ask for feedback from your participants. Whether it's a question people can answer in a chat, or a poll question, or through a quick pulse survey sent out electronically after the meeting, it's a good practice to hear what's working and what could be improved. This is easier in an in-person meeting but can be more challenging when you're working remotely.

New technologies, methodologies and virtual best practices are developing every day, so take advantage of the wisdom of your participants to crowdsource ways to make your virtual meetings even more productive.

## Take Action

### TRANSFER INGREDIENTS

**More of:**
- ☑ Walk your talk
- ☑ Take baby steps
- ☑ What needs to be different tomorrow?
- ☑ Decide who's doing what by when
- ☑ Iterate, Learn, Adapt, Repeat
- ☑ Make conversations visual

**Less of:**
- ☒ Pack the agenda
- ☒ Throw spaghetti
- ☒ Analysis paralysis
- ☒ Look for big leap next steps
- ☒ No follow-up communication or activity

**Add Your Own Ingredients:**
_____
_____
_____

**Watch Out For:**
_____
_____
_____

## ✅ Transfer Tactics Inventory

Do a quick inventory of strategies you can use to ensure the discussions and decisions from your meetings support execution and action-taking. Which of the following tactics would best serve you and your team?

- Share minutes post-meeting in a timely way
- Share any visual artifacts such as graphic recordings, outputs from group brainstorming activities and the chatbox
- Ensure action items are assigned to specific individuals, with a target due date
- Establish a follow-plan
- Create protocols for clear, timely communication flow between team members to support follow-up work
- Solicit feedback on the meeting to help support and plan future meeting agendas
- Other actions or structures to support your team's work getting done

## ✅ Do a Pre-Mortem Assessment

It's useful to reflect and analyse what might get in the way of your team's success. One way is to assume that the project or initiative fails. From that starting point, work backwards to figure out what could have created the failure. Research shows that using this prospective hindsight approach increases the ability to correctly identify reasons for future outcomes by 30 percent (Klein, 2007).

By identifying pitfalls in advance, you can more easily plan for mitigation strategies and new approaches before your work has a chance to go sideways and miss the mark. Here are some questions to guide your thinking. You can do this exercise on your own or, if working with your team, include it as a topic to discuss together.

What could go wrong with this initiative?

What do we need that we don't currently have?

What do we need that we already have available?

What am I most worried about?

_____

_____

_____

_____

What am I most excited about?

_____

_____

_____

_____

What lessons have I learned from past experience that would be helpful to apply now?

_____

_____

_____

_____

_____

CHAPTER EIGHT

# Handling Hybrid Meetings

*The reinvention of daily lives means marching off the edge of our maps.*

– Bob Black

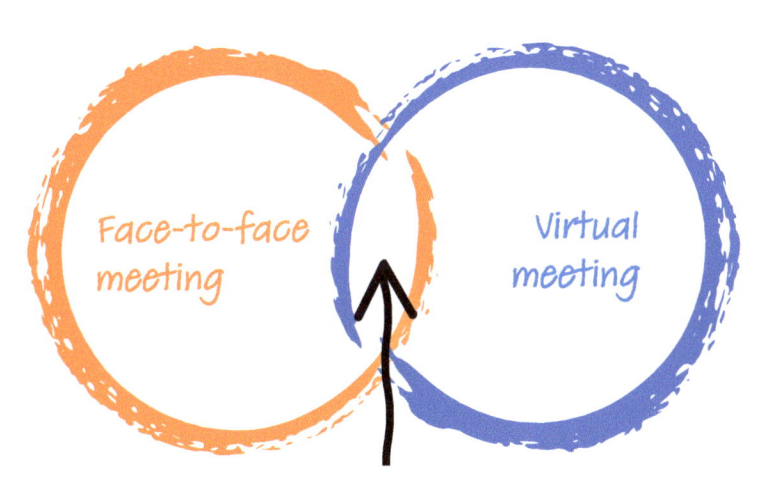

*Figure 11: Hybrid Meetings*

The learning COVID-19 has thrown at us will continue long after we find a way to prevent its spread and health risks. Before the pandemic, opportunities for employees to work remotely were more the exception than the rule. We have adapted quickly to working from home to comply with prescribed public health measures to contain the spread of the virus.

The next challenge facing busy managers will be how to effectively lead hybrid meetings, conversations or gatherings where some attendees are co-located in the same physical space while others participate using conferencing technology.

I've heard plenty of stories of how these are working (or not!). Here are a few examples:

- You kick off your next virtual meeting, only to discover that two participants have decided at the last minute to meet up in a co-working space – but without headphones. Instead of starting strongly with meaningful connection and clarity about the purpose of the meeting, you spend the first ten minutes troubleshooting audio feedback. It leaves all participants frustrated and feeling like their time is not respected.
- You're so relieved that meetings are returning to normal that you focus mainly on the attendees physically in the room. Your virtual attendees feel like ignored bystanders, as their chat comments or raised hands aren't consistently or effectively incorporated into the discussion.
- You have been leading a monthly meeting remotely, but now five group members are joining in from the office boardroom, while the rest continue to connect via videoconference. You find it much harder to read the room because it's difficult to see those five people in one small Zoom square.

- You notice far more sidebar conversations happening with the people who are physically in the same room. It creates a distraction for the virtual participants because they can't hear what's being said and feel left out of the loop.

Hybrid meetings take the connection challenge up a notch because the playing field for participant engagement is no longer level.

## Hybrid is Here to Stay

The pandemic has fundamentally shifted how and where we work together. Some businesses such as Shopify, Atlassian, Facebook and Dropbox, have decided that employees can work from home permanently (Courtney, 2021). Others are designing options for employees to work a specified number of days from home per week or per month, with policies that will necessitate hybrid meetings. According to the 2020 Global Workforce Survey, 98 percent of meetings will include at least one remote participant (Dimensional Research, 2020).

A survey of global executives conducted by MIT Sloan indicates that COVID-19 has driven a permanent shift in how we work with respondents expecting to continue to work virtually at least 50 percent of the time beyond the pandemic. Further, the survey notes an acceleration of a pre-COVID-19 shift in how individuals and teams do intellectual work. Routine tasks involving coordination and transactions can be effectively carried out in virtual meetings, but work requiring a deeper level of team collaboration, such as collective learning, innovation, or building a shared culture, is better accomplished face-to-face. The authors conclude that "the post-pandemic future of teamwork will be a purposefully hybrid combination of virtual coordination and in-person collaboration" (Hooijberg & Watkins, 2021).

The future workplace will undoubtedly require continued agility and responsiveness in how work is done. Just as nobody had a playbook for running an organization through a global pandemic, there is no clear checklist for working together post-pandemic. However, the roadmap to the next "normal" will best be developed through dialogue and consultation with all parts of the organization.

Shifting out of a predominantly virtual and work-from-home paradigm offers an opportunity to build upon the lessons learned and intentionally leave behind practices and processes that no longer serve the purpose of our meetings and gatherings.

Priya Parker, author of *The Art of Gathering: How We Meet and Why it Matters*, urges organizations to take advantage of this unique moment in time as we collectively emerge from the impacts of the COVID-19 pandemic. In a podcast interview with Brené Brown, Parker said, "Return is an opportunity to hit the reset button. Let's not rush back to formats that weren't working for us before. Pause and ask, "How do we want to do this now?" We need to have conversations about this" (Brown, 2021).

> We're in this extraordinary moment that resulted from a lot of pain and devastation, in which, at some level, the decks have been cleared. We can decide how we want to be together and what we want that to look like."
>
> – *Priya Parker*

In this chapter, we'll consider issues and practical tips you'll need to pay particular attention to when leading hybrid meetings. Let's look at them through the COUNT Roadmap.

## CALIBRATE

Running effective hybrid meetings can feel confronting and even overwhelming. Unless you are well prepared, the logistics of organizing a Conversation that Counts can swamp your sense of confidence and presence. Professors Hooijberg and Watkins advise that "Effective leadership in this new hybrid world requires different skills that go beyond traditional team leadership" (Hooijberg & Watkins, 2021). Your preparation takes on a new level of urgency and importance when leading a hybrid meeting. Consider these tips to help you get your head in the game.

### Decide the Best Way to Meet

Just because you can have a hybrid meeting doesn't mean that you should. With the complexity involved, double-check that what you're doing warrants the additional planning, technology and challenge. Does that daily huddle or weekly team planning session really need to be hybrid just because thirty percent of your team is scheduled to be in the office that day? Information sharing, reviewing progress and touching base could easily continue as a virtual gathering. It might be better to put that extra planning and effort into collaborative, strategic planning or culture-building endeavours, where the stakes are higher. Be discerning about trying to match up the kind of work you're doing with the type of meeting you need.

### Amp Up Your Mindset

Becoming a Conversation Leader who is adept at running meetings in all kinds of environments requires you to dig deep into personal resilience and willingness to stretch your comfort zone. As noted earlier, your energy and attitude set the tone for the entire group. Be willing to experiment and get input from your team about what would work for them. It's time to be humble and admit you're all in new territory. Normalize the discomfort and frustration that will undoubtedly arise as you all become better at this.

### 💡 Call for Backup

Managing participants together in in-person and virtual environments can make it hard to be present and pick up everyone's comments, concerns and dynamics. Deputize someone in the session to help you ensure all participants feel supported to participate on an equal footing. If you're in a room with others, deputize someone to watch the chat and keep an eye on the virtual participants.

With greater technological complexity, a meeting producer who handles the technology and connectivity, both for set-up and during the meeting, can relieve stress about tech glitches. Have a dry run to ensure your technology is going to work well. Make sure you have screens, so virtual participants are clearly seen in the room. Aside from the agenda, give each attendee a pre-meeting checklist so everyone is clear about which equipment, apps, or other tools will be used.

### ORIENT

You'll need to put yourself in the shoes of participants who are in your physical meeting room as well as those sitting behind a computer. Recognize that there will be some natural, spontaneous and infectious enthusiasm and camaraderie among face-to-face participants – particularly if they are still getting used to being in rooms with real people again!

However, your virtual participants need to feel fully part of the discussion and not just bystanders. "The real challenge in keeping a hybrid workforce energized is not technological or logistical, but emotional" (Knox, 2020).

Here are some tips to help you get oriented to the nuances of leading a hybrid meeting.

### 💡 Update Your Group Agreements

As discussed in Chapter Four, it's helpful to set clear expectations about how you want people to participate. These group agreements about behaviour need to be updated to meet the needs of a hybrid environment. Here are a few you might want to add:

- Ask everyone to keep their cameras on. When people are seen, they are more likely to feel heard, respected and able to participate.
- Ask in-person participants to speak to the camera and virtual participants, rather than solely to you as the meeting leader or to others around the board room. This will help keep clear audio and ensure remote attendees feel part of the group.
- Limit cross-talk. Sidebar conversations often happen in person but can be distracting and create a sense of disconnection with remote participants.

### 💡 Know Who is Where

Be sure to find out in advance how people will be joining your meeting. This will avoid any last-minute surprises that may impact your technology requirements, audio-visual aids or other ways you want people to work together. If people are together, ask them to speak up and to the camera to make a connection with their fellow virtual colleagues – not just to those in the room.

### 💡 Ask for Input

Before the meeting, find out what participants need to feel fully supported and able to participate. Don't assume that just because everyone became adept at virtual meetings, they will be ready for the different dynamics of a hybrid arrangement. Ask what support they need and check during the meeting to see if any issues have emerged. For example, someone might be blocking their camera view or need to speak louder to be heard.

## UNDERSTAND

It is critical to ensure equity in participation to make everyone feels included and has a sense of belonging. Working virtually somewhat democratized our meeting participation during the pandemic, with more opportunities such as chat discussion and breakout rooms. This has seen less outspoken employees finding it easier to share their ideas than with in-person meetings (Weishaupt, 2021).

As Priya Parker commented to Brené Brown, "Restructuring meetings to allow for true hybrid participation brings up a lot of questions around power and access" (Brown, 2021). Using these tips will help you ensure that remote and in-person participants are on an equal footing.

### 💡 Open with an Equal Playing Field

When soliciting views from your team, consider using virtual interactive tools to gather their input rather than asking people to raise their hands and share. Facilitation expert, Rae Ringel, advises that "Technology is an essential part of hybrid meetings, but it shouldn't be looked at as something for the remote employee only. Instead, normalize the use of digital meeting tools for everyone" (Ringel, 2021).

Some interactive tools I find helpful are Mentimeter and Slido. These tools allow you to engage participants through poll questions, creating word clouds, surveys and quizzes, and more. Similarly, using virtual tools like Mural or Miro, rather than flipcharts, for brainstorming or whiteboard activities ensures that everyone has equal access to information and can contribute.

By sharing identical platforms, you can hear from everyone equally, and they can see the range of views on the table together.

### 💡 Engage Virtual Participants First

Engage your virtual participants right from the start to help them feel emotionally connected and engaged. Whether by greeting them personally as they pop on to your monitor or turning to remote participants first when opening up a discussion, ensure you consistently bring attention to that group. Eye contact through the camera is especially important.

### 💡 Mix Up Your Breakout Rooms

Logistically, small group discussions may seem simpler with virtual participants in Zoom or Teams breakout rooms and in-person participants huddled in parts of the physical room. But if you're keeping the quality of relationships at the forefront, you'll mix up breakout discussions across both groups. It might mean on-site participants need to grab a laptop and head to someone's office to join a virtual breakout space, but fostering true hybrid collaboration right down to small group discussions continues to send the vital message that you regard everyone's participation inclusively and equitably.

## NAVIGATE

Dealing with challenging issues or personalities that erupt in a meeting is not something that most of us look forward to. Handling these is even harder in a hybrid situation – particularly when the environment is not well constructed and already feels somewhat chaotic. Here are some strategies to keep in mind when you navigate the tough stuff in a hybrid meeting.

### Check Your Expectations

Allow extra time in your hybrid agenda. If you think a discussion should only take 15-20 minutes, plan for 30 minutes instead. There are many transitions between technologies required to support hybrid facilitation. It takes people time to find their breakout rooms or get their polling tool loaded into a new browser window. Your virtual participants may be handling distractions or other demands on their attention if working from home. These will likely be quite different or even absent for your in-person participants. Leave even more space in your agenda so you don't add excessive time pressures on your participants and lead to tempers flaring.

### Hit the Pause Button

If a complicated issue arises that threatens to derail things, you may have to hit the pause button. Rather than getting stuck in a debate with one opinionated person, create a quick poll and ask the group for their perspectives on the issue at hand. This brings in all the voices in the room and can shift the dynamic from an emerging tit-for-tat argument. In some cases, you might decide a sidebar conversation with a sub-group of people is needed, so have everyone else go for a stretch while you hop into a breakout room to discuss the matter.

## TRANSFER

Ensuring the ideas, decisions and momentum of the meeting are transferred into action are just as important and needed in a hybrid session. These strategies can help you.

### 💡 Keeping the Record Straight

Creating and using visual artifacts, working on collaborative documents, keeping a record of the chat and using that as a source of knowledge are incredibly valuable. These collaborative outputs can be seen and developed by all participants and ensure equal visibility and participation in the meeting outcome. Many of us fine-tuned best practices for collaboration during the pandemic, and these are great to bring into the next normal in the workplace.

### 💡 Commit to Continuous Improvement

Self-reflection is essential to the growing competence and confidence of people who want to lead Conversations that Count, yet we all have blind spots. Conduct a regular post-meeting feedback survey on how all participants felt about working together in the session. Consider how actual participation transpired in comparison with how you'd hoped it would go. Ask how the technology supported or distracted from the quality of the discussion and meeting outcome?

Having a committed habit of review and feedback about what worked well, what didn't and what could be improved next time allows you to keep building and iterating effective hybrid meetings and Conversations that Count with your team.

**Take Action**

### HANDLING HYBRID MEETINGS

**More of:**
- ☑ Pick right format for meeting purpose
- ☑ Get back-up support
- ☑ Pre-meeting prep for all participants
- ☑ Level playing field to create equitable opporunities and connection

Add Your Own Ingredients:
_____
_____
_____
_____

**Less of:**
- ☒ Focus and attention on in-person participants
- ☒ Ignoring remote participants
- ☒ Cross talk
- ☒ Being a lone ranger and doing it all on your own
- ☒ Not having back-up plans

Watch Out For:
_____
_____
_____
_____

### ✓ Assess Your Readiness

When planning for a meeting with participants who will be both in-person and remote, honestly assess your capability and readiness to lead a hybrid Conversation that Counts. Consider these key questions:

- **Technology:** Do you have the audio and video capability for participants to hear and see one another fully? This includes ensuring your remote participants can understand what's happening in the physical meeting room and bringing in remote participants via large monitors or screens.

- **Where are your people:** Are you clear on how people will participate in the session? Have they had proper guidance about how to prepare and connect?
- **Support team:** Who can support you by ensuring your tech is working properly? And who can be an extra pair of eyes and ears for you in reading the room? Many hands make light work, so be sure you have the support that will enable you to focus fully on leading the discussion.
- **Plan for Engagement:** When running a hybrid meeting, it's crucial to get the participant voice in the room and have a way to hear from them directly. Use virtual collaboration tools like Mentimeter, Slido or others to help you get input from people so you can all see the results together, and then go deeper on your discussion from there.
- **Ask Your Participants:** Conduct a pre- and post-session survey of all participants to find out what they need to be successful in working together in a hybrid meeting. What worked, what didn't, and what could be improved for next time? This is new territory for most, so design, iterate and improve how you run your hybrid meeting with the input from your team.

# PART THREE
# YOUR NEXT STEPS

Now it's time to put it all together. As I've said, information without action is useless. Information with action becomes wisdom. I don't want you to have come this far and not given you one final tool to readily put what you've learned into action, in a way that feels authentic and true to you.

In Part 3 we're going to zoom back out and walk through the COUNT Roadmap. This is an activity you can review and complete in ten minutes, before you start the meeting.

The COUNT Roadmap is how you prepare yourself to show up as a fully present, resilient and inspiring leader of the discussion.

CHAPTER NINE

# Your COUNT Roadmap

*Ideas are useless unless used. The proof of their value is in their implementation. Until then, they are in limbo.*

– *Theodore Levitt*

Let's make sure that the idea of leading Conversations that Count doesn't evaporate into the ether or become just another piece of data adding to your already taxed cognitive load, shall we? It's important to take steps to integrate the principles in this book and get your feet wet by using the COUNT framework in the meetings and discussions you lead. I always find a roadmap useful to get from where I am to where I want to go. Here's yours.

# COUNT Roadmap

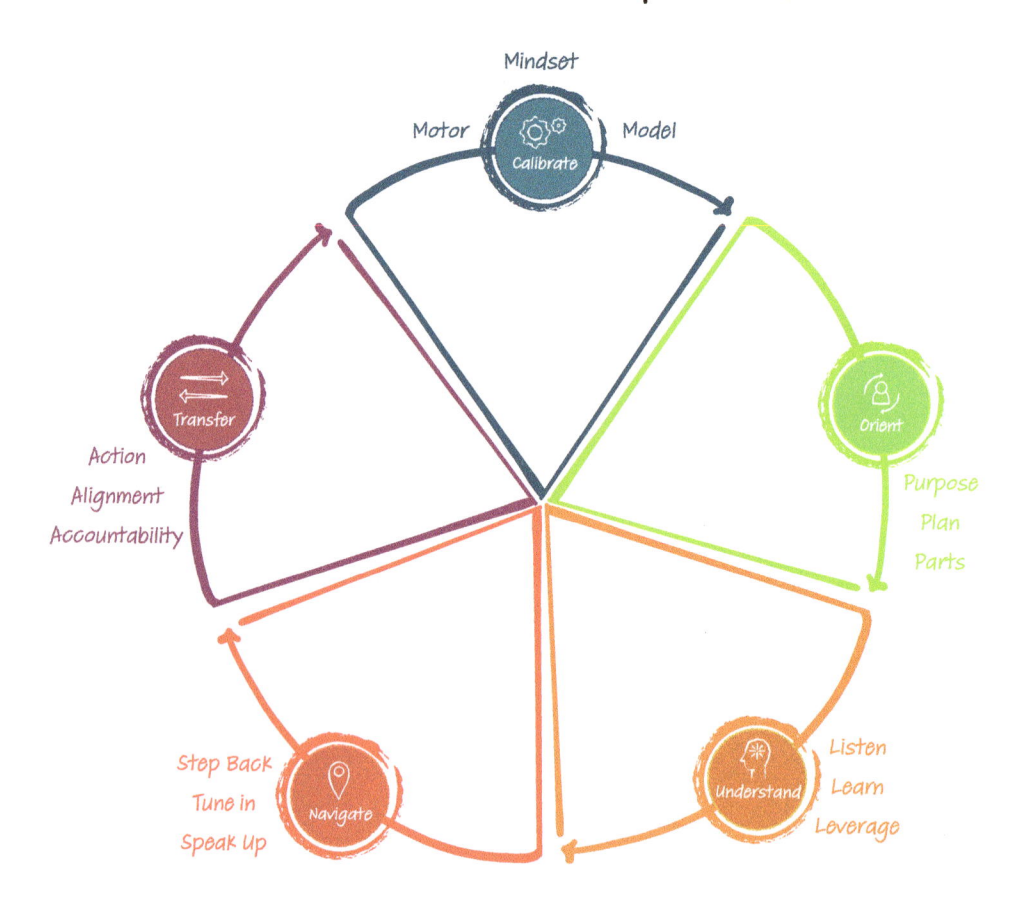

- Calibrate: Mindset, Motor, Model
- Orient: Purpose, Plan, Parts
- Understand: Listen, Learn, Leverage
- Navigate: Step Back, Tune In, Speak Up
- Transfer: Action, Alignment, Accountability

## SELF-REFLECTION

| What worked? | What didn't? | Do differently next time? |

*Figure 11: Your COUNT Roadmap*

## Create Your Own COUNT Roadmap

Use the COUNT Roadmap above as a template to help get in the right mindset and presence to lead an impactful meeting. To download a pdf copy of the roadmap, visit www.LeadConversationsThatCount.com

Let's walk through it, using our Chapter One story about Tom and the breakout discussion he's about to lead fixing employee participation at his company.

Before Tom gets to the room, he grabs a blank copy of the COUNT Roadmap. He already knows the subject matter and agenda parameters he has to work with, but Tom wants to be in peak condition as Conversation Leader. Even with a packed schedule and little time, Tom knows that taking ten minutes to reflect and make notes on his COUNT Roadmap will pay off enormously in leading the meeting and drawing the best from the team discussion. You'll see Tom's completed COUNT Roadmap in Figure 12.

The first stop on his map is **Calibrate**. Tom knows that how he shows up in terms of his mindset and presence has a big impact on his group. People will follow his lead. He takes deep breaths and starts to tune in to his own physical and emotional signals. He feels pressure to get useful solutions from the discussion. Poor execution, flagging productivity levels and the changing work environment are some of the things that have recently been keeping him up at night. His internal critic has been pretty active, telling him his recent promotion was a fluke and blaming his superiors for not giving him enough direction. He jots down, "Leave my critic at the door," as a reminder to park these issues so he can be present.

Tom has received feedback that while he's great at solving problems, he sometimes misses important nuances because he can drive to fix things first rather than understand them deeply. Tom knows that staying curious longer, and asking more questions rather than rushing to provide answers, will help him. He makes a note to "Be curious" and "Ask more, talk less". He writes these two prompts on separate sticky notes and puts them next to his computer to remind himself during the meeting.

Tom also knows he can be like a dog with a bone when confronted with unexpected problems. He writes "Bend my knees" as a reminder to show up like a surfer, so he's balanced and ready for any challenge. Tom chuckles, thinking that if anyone reads these notes, they might be confused about their meaning. But he knows this COUNT Roadmap is just for him, and the act of walking through the various stages of the map is already helping him feel more confident and even excited about leading this high-stakes discussion.

Next, Tom moves to the **Orient** stage to create an intention for the experience he wants his participants to have. He imagines himself in his colleagues' shoes and considers what they might be thinking. There are a few new members of the team, so they may wonder if they made the right choice to join the company given the serious issues of engagement and a lack of innovation. Tom knows it's essential for them to feel part of the solution, so he writes down "Everyone's voice matters" to sum up his intention for folks to leave the meeting feeling safe and supported to contribute their ideas and questions. He also wants people to understand better the complexities of their work environment, so he writes down "Connect the dots". If everyone leaves the meeting feeling connected and with a clearer understanding of the big picture, Tom figures they will be better positioned to come up with solutions and feel a sense of commitment to turning the engagement challenge around.

In the **Understand** stage, Tom reflects on what he needs to do to really listen and communicate well in the discussion. He prides himself on being a quick thinker, able to draw accurate conclusions. This is a great skill and served him well in his previous role in data architecture with a small team of computer engineers and coders. But in Tom's new role of leading people, he has learned that his skills about making a quick assessment and moving ahead don't translate well when the data points he's analyzing are people. He's jumped to a few erroneous conclusions about people's priorities and perspectives, and it's caused some friction. Tom writes down "Help me to understand…" and "And what else?" because these two prompts help him listen better and encourage people to share more. He writes down "Silence is golden" to remind him to set aside the discomfort he feels when there's a lull in the discussion.

Next, Tom goes to **Navigate** to map out his game plan for when the group hits a rough patch or conflict in the meeting. He notes "A toxin-free zone" as a reminder to keep an eye out and address any toxic behaviour that arises. He also writes down "Dance floor to the balcony" so he remembers to shift his perspective to get a clearer understanding of any challenging group dynamics that may arise.

Finally, Tom thinks about how important it is to keep the momentum of the discussion going after the meeting is over. In the **Transfer** box, he writes, "What's the one thing you'll do?" that he'll use as a prompt question for people to respond to as a way to take action. Since the meeting is virtual, Tom decides to ask that in the chat and take a few shares. He adds "Chatbox, then share out" to remember how he wants to run that important part of the discussion. As a follow-up, he'll make sure the chat conversation is shared, and send a summary to everyone after the meeting, asking them to let him know how they are doing with their actions in a week's time. He writes down "One-week follow-up" on the roadmap.

Tom takes a last look over his roadmap and smiles. "What do you know?" he muses. "That looks like a great and very doable plan!" By filling in each area of the map with choices that feel authentic and important to Tom and his communication style, he feels a great sense of relief. Before he did this, he would often feel he was winging it in meetings. Now, Tom feels a greater sense of freedom and clarity about how he needs to show up. He feels confident that this meeting will be impactful and important for everyone. He'll run it so that relationships are strengthened, and the team will be more empowered and clearer on the steps they need to take. Tom feels excited, confident and ready to lead a Conversation that Counts.

**Self-Reflection After the Meeting**

Part of the COUNT Roadmap is an area for **self-reflection**. Within a few hours of the meeting ending, Tom pulled out his COUNT Roadmap to complete this final section. He felt great about how the meeting went, and planned to take a few minutes to reflect on what worked, what didn't work so well, and how he'd approach things differently for his next meeting.

Tom started with the "What worked?" section. He was very happy with the prompt "Help me to understand…" and noticed it worked well in the meeting. He only used it a couple of times when someone made a point that wasn't clear to him or the group. It felt very natural to say that, so he decides he'll keep that one at the top of his Conversations that Count toolkit. Having people use the chat to answer the "What's one thing you'll do?" question at the end was very well received! People told him they wanted the chat summary of everyone's ideas, and it made good use of the time. Tom made a note to use this format in future meetings because it also helped build connections and fostered relationships.

Shifting to the "What didn't work?" section, Tom realized the opening could have been smoother. Some people arrived at the video conference a few minutes early, but he wasn't quite ready, so he just smiled at them and stayed silent. Tom felt the start of the meeting was a bit sluggish, and it took the group a bit longer than he had hoped to warm up and talk to each other.

Thinking about what he would do differently next time, Tom made a note to plan for a better start. Even though the meeting officially started at a certain time, Tom decided he'd be more prepared for early arrivals, engaging with them and asking a few questions about how things were going for them. He wanted to demonstrate that he cared about them, so modelling empathy, curiosity and connection before the meeting got underway was something he decided to try out next time.

In as little as 10 minutes, you can chart your course through the COUNT Roadmap and shift the way you lead your next meeting. By using this methodology, I have no doubt you'll create an environment where your team shows up eager, committed and willing to give their best creativity and solutions to the issues you face. Boring, frustrating and unproductive meetings will be a thing of the past when you're leading them. This framework helps you to demystify the world of group dynamics and develop concrete strategies and intentions for yourself so you can lead Conversations that Count.

# Tom's COUNT Roadmap

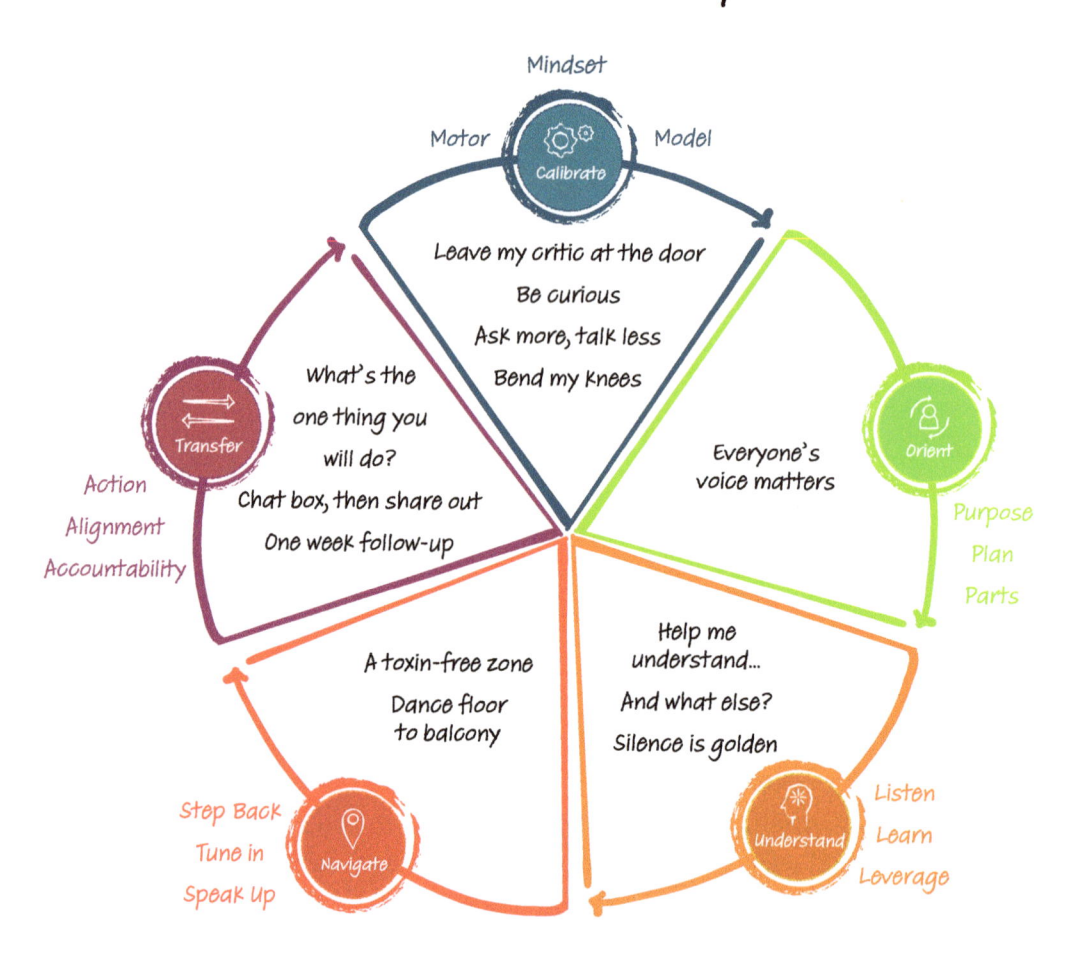

**Calibrate**
- Motor
- Mindset
- Model

Leave my critic at the door
Be curious
Ask more, talk less
Bend my knees

**Orient**
- Purpose
- Plan
- Parts

Everyone's voice matters

**Understand**
- Listen
- Learn
- Leverage

Help me understand...
And what else?
Silence is golden

**Navigate**
- Step Back
- Tune in
- Speak Up

A toxin-free zone
Dance floor to balcony

**Transfer**
- Action
- Alignment
- Accountability

What's the one thing you will do?
Chat box, then share out
One week follow-up

## SELF-REFLECTION

**What worked?**
What's one thing you'll do?
Worked great!

**What didn't?**
Opening could have been smoother – felt sluggish.

**Do differently next time?**
Start earlier and chat before meeting

Figure 12: Tom's Completed COUNT Roadmap

# Work With Me

Thank you for reading *Lead Conversations that Count*! I appreciate your decision to spend time reading and absorbing the information presented here.

My intention in writing this book is to give busy managers important principles and practical tools to ditch boring meetings and create a meaningful, impactful dialogue with their team that helps them all do great work together. Do you now feel able to create your own roadmap to engaging and inspiring discussions?

I would love to hear how it's working for you as you implement these strategies. Please feel free to drop me an email or let's connect on LinkedIn.

Please visit **www.LeadConversationsThatCount.com** for more templates, tips and tools to help you in your journey.

If you would like more support – for yourself or your organization, I offer a variety of training, facilitation and coaching programs. To learn more or inquire, visit **www.LeadConversationsThatCount.com**

If you have any questions, please reach out. I would love to connect!

Here's to unleashing your brilliance in the world!

*Caitlin Ellis*

www.BrillianceMastery.com
hello@BrillianceMastery.com

# About the Author

I've always been fascinated by maps, and through Brilliance Mastery, I'm like a modern-day cartographer. I help corporate and organizational clients navigate from where they are to where they need to be to achieve meaningful and measurable success. I help clients spark new insights and learning, foster collaboration and meaningful relationships, and build buy-in to take action. This is reflected in my passion for helping my clients make sense of the complexities and challenges they face.

I have more than 20 years of experience in the public and entrepreneurial sectors, with 15 of those years working in transformational leadership. With a Masters in Public Policy from Harvard's Kennedy School of Government, I have worked on Wall Street, as a senior policy advisor in the Ontario government, and as a Director of Development for two of Canada's most prestigious independent schools.

I have an insatiable curiosity and a commitment to lifelong learning, with a highly interdisciplinary and holistic approach to problem-solving. I have trained extensively with CRR Global in Organizational and Relationship System Coaching (ORSC ™) and Grove Consultants International in Strategic Visioning and Team Performance.

I read science fiction in my spare time and am a member of The Riverdale Players – a community musical theatre troupe in my hometown of Toronto, Ontario. The organization raises funds to support at-risk children and provide teacher training in impoverished villages in Africa and with First Nations communities in Canada. I'm the mom of three amazing young adults and one fluffy, bouncy golden doodle.

# Gratitude

It takes a village to birth a book, and I am deeply grateful to the many villagers who offered their support, insights, and encouragement.

To my incredible clients, colleagues and thought partners, I thank you for working and playing over the years. We've had rich conversations together about the huge changes we face, what we need to do differently, individually and collectively, and we've remembered we are truly all in this together.

I am deeply grateful to my parents, Jack and Barbara Ellis, for your unfailing love and support. You taught me from an early age to appreciate that no matter where we live, the languages we speak, or the cultures in which we were raised, it's important to find a way to respect, connect and learn from those who may have a different perspective.

To Erin, Kyle and Matthew – I couldn't be more proud of the amazing adults you have become. Thank you for your strength, encouragement, and ability to make me laugh.

# References

Andrew, D., 2018. *Who's to Blame? 94% Chance It's a System Failure, Not You.* [Online]
Available at: https://medium.com/the-mission/whos-to-blame-94-chance-it-s-a-system-failure-not-you-26396b2b3811

Ashkenas, R., 2015. *To Lead Change, Explain the Context.* [Online]
Available at: https://hbr.org/2015/11/to-lead-change-explain-the-context

Berman, R., 2020. *New study suggests we have 6,200 thoughts every day.* [Online]
Available at: https://bigthink.com/mind-brain/how-many-thoughts-per-day?rebelltitem=1#rebelltitem1

Bowden, M., 2021. *Building Presence and Connection via Zoom.* s.l., s.n.

Brown, B., 2015. *Daring Greatly: How the Courage to Be Vulnerable Transforms the Way We Live, Love, Parent, and Lead.* New York: Avery.

Chartwell Content, 2017. *6 Ways to Overcome the Forgetting Curve.* [Online]
Available at: https://medium.com/@CWContent/6-ways-to-overcome-the-forgetting-curve-354151c355c

Covey, S., 1989. *The Seven Habits of Highly Effective People.* New York: Simon and Schuster.

Covey, S. R., n.d. *Habit 2: Begin with the End in Mind.* [Online]
Available at: https://genius.com/Stephen-r-covey-habit-2-begin-with-the-end-in-mind-annotated

Deloitte, 2016. *The 2016 Deloitte Millennial Survey: Winning Over the Next Generation of Leaders.* [Online]
Available at: https://www2.deloitte.com/content/dam/Deloitte/global/Documents/About-Deloitte/gx-millenial-survey-2016-exec-summary.pdf

Dempsey, L., 2019. *Meeting Stats That May Surprise You.* [Online]
Available at: https://www.cornerstonedynamics.com/meeting-stats-that-may-surprise-you/

Dweck, C., 2007. *Mindset: The New Psychology of Success.* New York: Ballantine Books.

Edmondson, A. C., 2019. *The Fearless Organization: Creating Psychological Safety in the Workplace for Learning, Innovation, and Growth.* Hoboken, New Jersey: John Wiley & Sons.

Gallup, 2020. *The State of the American Manager,* Washington, DC: Gallup.

*Ghostbusters.* 1984. [Film] Directed by I. Reitman. USA: Columbia Pictures.

Gregerson, H., 2018. *Questions are the Answer: A Breakthrough Approach to Your Most Vexing Problems at Work and In Life.* New York: HarperBusiness.

*Groundhog Day.* 1993. [Film] Directed by Harold Ramis, George Fenton, Sharon Boyle, Jeff Atmajian. USA: Columbia Pictures.

Hanson, R., Kornfield, J. & Mendius, R., 2009. *Buddha's Brain: The Practical Neuroscience of Happiness, Love and Wisdom.* Oakland: New Harbinger Publications.

Heifetz, R. A. & Linsky, M., 2009. *Practice of Adaptive Leadership: Tools and Tactics for Changing Your Organization and the World.* Boston: Harvard Business Review Press.

Heifetz, R. & Linsky, M., 2002. *A Survival Guide for Leaders.* [Online]
Available at: https://hbr.org/2002/06/a-survival-guide-for-leaders

Jiang, M., 2020. *The Reason Zoom Calls Drain Your Energy.* [Online]
Available at: https://www.bbc.com/worklife/article/20200421-why-zoom-video-chats-are-so-exhausting

Kaner, S., 2014. *Facilitator's Guide to Participatory Decision-Making.* 3rd ed. San Francisco: Jossey-Bass.

Katrin Schoenenberg, A. R. J. K., 2014. Why are you so slow? - Misattribution of transmission delay to attributes of the conversation partner at the far-end. *International Journal of Human-Computer Studies,* pp. 477-487.

Keith, E., 2015. *55 million: A fresh look at the number, effectiveness, and cost of meetings in the U.S..* [Online]
Available at: https://blog.lucidmeetings.com/blog/fresh-look-number-effectiveness-cost-meetings-in-us

Klein, G., 2007. *Performing a Project Premortem.* [Online]
Available at: https://hbr.org/2007/09/performing-a-project-premortem

Knight, R., 2018. *Tips for Reading the Room before a Meeting or Presentation.* [Online]
Available at: https://hbr.org/2018/05/tips-for-reading-the-room-before-a-meeting-or-presentation

Lee, J., 2020. *A Neurophysiological Exploration of Zoom Fatigue.* [Online]
Available at: https://www.psychiatrictimes.com/view/psychological-exploration-zoom-fatigue

Leong, T., 2020. *VUCA 2.0 in the current COVID-19 outbreak.* [Online]
Available at: http://www.focusadventure.com/vuca-2-0-in-the-current-covid-19-outbreak/

Leslie A. Perlow, C. N. H. E. E., 2017. *Stop the Meeting Madness - How to free up time for meaningful work.* [Online]
Available at: https://hbr.org/2017/07/stop-the-meeting-madness

Martin, M., 2020. *The State of Meetings in 2020*. [Online]
Available at: https://bettermeetings.expert/MEETING-STATISTICS/

May, C., 2014. *A Learning Secret: Don't Take Notes with a Laptop*. [Online]
Available at: https://www.scientificamerican.com/article/a-learning-secret-don-t-take-notes-with-a-laptop/

McIntyre, D. R., 2021. *Understanding Pandemic Burnout* [Interview] (12 April 2021).

Merriam-Webster, n.d. *Calibrate definition*. [Online]
Available at: https://www.merriam-webster.com/dictionary/calibrate

Miller, J., 2016. *The great goldfish attention span myth - and why it's killing content marketing*. [Online]
Available at: https://business.linkedin.com/marketing-solutions/blog/best-practices--content-marketing/2016/the-great-goldfish-attention-span-myth--and-why-its-killing-cont

Mind Tools, 2018. *The COIN Conversation Model: Taking the Sting out of Difficult Feedback*. [Online]
Available at: https://www.mindtools.com/pages/article/COIN.htm

Molla, R., 2020. *The pandemic was great for Zoom. What happens when there's a vaccine?*. [Online]
Available at: https://www.vox.com/recode/21726260/zoom-microsoft-teams-video-conferencing-post-pandemic-coronavirus

Newport, C., 2016. *Deep Work: Rules for Focused Success in a Distracted World*. New York: Grand Central Publishing.

Newport, C., 2019. *Digital Minimalism: Choosing a Focused Life in a Noisy World*. New York: Portfolio.

Oxfam International, 2020. *World's billionaires have more wealth than 4.6 billion people*. [Online]

Available at: https://www.oxfam.org/en/press-releases/worlds-billionaires-have-more-wealth-46-billion-people

Parker, P., 2018. *The Art of Gathering: How We Meet and Why it Matters.* New York: Riverhead Books.

Parvez, H., 2015. *Body language: Head and neck gestures.* [Online]
Available at: https://www.psychmechanics.com/body-language-gestures-of-head-and-neck/

Pasricha, N., 2016. *The Happiness Equation: Want Nothing + Do Anything = Have Everything.* New York: Penguin Random House.

Perlow, L. A., Hadley, C. N. & Eun, E., 2017. *Stop the Meeting Madness.* [Online]
Available at: https://hbr.org/2017/07/stop-the-meeting-madness

Peterson-Withorn, C., 2020. *The World's Billionaries Have Gotten $1.9 Trillion Richer in 2020.* [Online]
Available at: https://www.oxfam.org/en/press-releases/worlds-billionaires-have-more-wealth-46-billion-people

Porter, J., 2017. *Why You Should Make Time for Self-Reflection (Even If You Hate Doing It).* [Online]
Available at: https://hbr.org/2017/03/why-you-should-make-time-for-self-reflection-even-if-you-hate-doing-it

Purdue University Global, n.d. *Generational Differences in the Workplace.* [Online]
Available at: https://www.purdueglobal.edu/education-partnerships/generational-workforce-differences-infographic/

Reed, K. M. & Allen, J. A., 2021. *Suddenly Virtual: Making Remote Meetings Work.* New York: Wiley.

*Saturday Night Fever.* 1977. [Film] Directed by John Badham. USA: Paramount Pictures.

Schwartz, R., 2016. 5 Ways Meetings Get Off Track, and How to Prevent Each One. *Harvard Business Review.*

Scott, E., 2020. *The Toxic Effects of Negative Self-Talk.* [Online]
 Available at: https://www.verywellmind.com/negative-self-talk-and-how-it-affects-us-4161304

Sibbett, D., 2021. *Pioneering Visual and Virtual Practices for Collaboration.* [Online]
 Available at: https://www.thegrove.com

Strategy&, 2013. *Culture's Role in Enabling Organizational Change.* [Online]
 Available at: https://www.strategyand.pwc.com/gx/en/insights/2011-2014/cultures-role-organizational-change.html

Volini, E., Schwartz, J. & Eaton, K., 2020. *Deloitte Insights: Human Capital Trends 2021,* London: Deloitte.

Wikipedia, 2021. *Forgetting curve.* [Online]
 Available at: https://en.wikipedia.org/wiki/Forgetting_curve

Wikipedia, 2021. *Wicked Problem.* [Online]
 Available at: https://en.wikipedia.org/wiki/Wicked_problem

Wise, W. & Littlefield, C., 2017. *Ask Power Questions - Create Conversations that Matter.* Seattle: CreateSpace Independent Publishing Platform.

Wong, K., 2019. *Why You Can't Afford Disengaged Employees.* [Online]
 Available at: https://www.achievers.com/blog/why-you-cant-afford-disengaged-employees/

World Economic Forum, 2020. *These are the top 10 job skills of tomorrow - and how long it takes to learn them.* [Online]
 Available at: https://www.weforum.org/agenda/2020/10/top-10-work-skills-of-tomorrow-how-long-it-takes-to-learn-them/

CPSIA information can be obtained
at www.ICGtesting.com
Printed in the USA
LVHW071757270721
693851LV00021B/479

9 781777 707903